W9-ASV-923

GAMBLE AND WIN

GAMBLE AND WIN

JACK HART

GAMBLER'S BOOK CLUB
Las Vegas, Nevada

Published 1963 by
Onsco Publications
Hollywood, California

Standard Book Number: 911996-25-7

GAMBLER'S BOOK CLUB PREFACE

Jack Hart's GAMBLE AND WIN was originally published in 1963. G.B.C. listed the book in their 1964 catalog. It immediately became a best seller. Shortly after the 1971 catalog was issued GAMBLE AND WIN went out-of-print. Many people were disappointed.

Available now as one of a continuing series of Gambler's Book Club Reprints, the book becomes a permanent addition alongside other classics.

There's a shortage of good material about games of chance. Everything obtainable should be read by persons interested in the subject. As a reader you're not required to agree with the author's words. There are few subjects as controversial as gambling. But imagine the result if, with the reading of this book, only one idea is put to use and it reduces losses 5%; or even better, the gambling profits can be increased 5% or more. Regardless of which happens, learning at the gaming table, without some help, can be very expensive. And speaking of expense, the bargain prices mentioned in Chapter 16 should be increased from 50 to 100 percent.

CONTENTS

CONTENTS

FOREWORD

"Jack Hart" is, quite obviously, not my own name. The reason I don't dare use my name is because when I gamble, I play from the same side of the table as you do. I am not a gambler by trade but I am closely associated with the gambling industry as a sort of unofficial "betting commissioner."

I'm the fellow who sets the odds on boxing, baseball, basketball, football — you name it. The odds on the four or five most popular forms of gambling, however, do not require the services of a "commissioner." The reason for this is that these odds, with only slight exceptions, are constant. In other words, the "house" always has an edge on you.

I positively will not guarantee you any foolproof system that will enable you to win *consistently*. There are plenty of chumps in this world, people we call "marks" or "chasers," who answer those phoney ads you see sprinkled throughout the newspapers, which guarantee you a foolproof system for winning at dice, or "How to Beat the Horses," or the roulette wheel, and so on. All this for only two dollars, (mailed to a postal box number!).

Let me assure you, my friends, there are no completely foolproof systems!

This book, however, will tell you how to cut your losses sharply. It will at least give you a half-way decent chance to walk away from the casinos with a profit.

Unlike many books on this subject, I am not going to take up space quoting the names of well-known celebrities, many of them known to me personally, who have won or lost sums of money far beyond the reach of the average person. Because, the vast majority of gamblers (non-professional) who come to the casinos in Las Vegas, two, three or four times a year, are small bettors, with perhaps a two or three hundred dollar bankroll.

This book is written for them.

While I do not care to engage in head-to-head gambling with people such as Edward O. Thorp, Mike Goodman, Mike McDougall, or John Scarn, I defy any one of these men to prove me wrong in the statements made in this book regarding odds, best systems for winning, and, above all, the best system for cutting your losses, and getting more pleasure from your gambling dollar.

Chapter I

"GAMES TO PLAY — GAMES NOT TO PLAY"

Over twenty million people pass through Las Vegas and Reno every year. Of this number possibly two-thirds are "over-nighters", people who stop on their way to or from the West Coast and say "Well, why don't we drop fifty bucks while we're here? We can tell the folks back home we gambled with the big shots in Las Vegas (or Reno) on our way out to Aunt Mamie's in Inglewood."

So, they drive out to the Strip where the enormous size of the casinos and clubs overawes them, then usually beat a hasty retreat back to Fremont Street in downtown Las Vegas. Here, the clubs are less formal and the action fast and furious. The players here play for considerably less money. Many of the clubs have a craps table, a twenty-one table and a roulette wheel, merely as courtesy. All of their action is on the slot machines.

There is only one sure way to beat a slot machine, but I don't advocate this system,—steal it and take it home with you.

Someone has started a legend that all slot machines in the State of Nevada must pay "so much" or "so much" and retain only a certain percentage for the house.

There is no such law in the State of Nevada. There is *no* law which compels the operator of a slot machine to pay off any amount, other than that of his own choosing. It's quite customary for a house to have its own mechanic set the slots to pay off a minimum figure over a busy weekend. Then on Monday, he resets them to pay off more liberally. Some clubs (which cater largely to women and do a large volume) claim they take a mark-up of only seven or eight percent. Others will work on a ten to fifteen percent mark-up.

Remember, these are claims only.

No one but the club owners are aware of how much percentage their machines earn. This is strictly legal and strictly, as I mentioned before, up to the owners. They, after all, are the men who must decide how much their slots must earn for them, in order to conduct a successful and profitable operation. And the necessary pay offs can differ greatly.

Remember, most of the clubs are open twenty-four hours a day, three hundred and sixty-five days a year.

They must therefore maintain three complete shifts of employees in addition to other overhead, so you can see that even the smallest of them is an expensive operation.

However, as long as you suckers continue to play slot machines, or "the one-armed bandits", the way you've been doing for the past fifty or sixty years, these people can stay in business, showing a handsome profit, meanwhile dispensing "free" souvenirs, "free"' food, and "free" booze. They can well afford it, you're footing the bill!

Why, then, is this — the one game which *can't* be beaten by the player—so popular?

From my observations, and from having watched the action around the slots for many years, I've observed plenty, I've arrived at two prime conclusions.

First, it doesn't take brains, or thought, to put your money in a slot machine, pull down the handle, and cross your fingers as the reels click. Since most slot machine players, or as I would call them "addicts", are of the female gender and feel that they cannot possibly lose the family fortune at a nickle or a dime a crack, most slot machines in Vegas are either nickle or dime machines. Although of course you can find plenty of quarter, half-dollar and silver dollar slot machines as well.

Second, after the poor chump has invested two or three dollars in a club featuring slots and hears the cry "Jackpot!" go up every four or five minutes, the particular machine he or she is playing becomes a mechanical metal enemy. He or she is determined to defeat it —to go for the jackpot. They frequently go broke during the battle.

If it's a ten dollar jackpot and it costs him "Only fifty or sixty dollars" to hit it, his warcry of "Jackpot!" is a triumphant one still. Sweaty and disheveled as he may be, with a right hand that looks as if he'd been shovelling coal (which happens when you pull that handle so much) he is happy. He has once again shown that *man is master* over all machinery!

On a slot machine with three reels there are either twenty or twenty-one "symbols" on each of these reels. The odds are eight thousand to one against hitting the jackpot on a three reel machine with *"only twenty* symbols per reel", and over nine thousand to one on a three slot with *"only twenty-one* symbols per reel".

Add a fourth reel, and the odds really get good! A mere hundred and sixty thousand to one against hitting the jackpot! Some of the clubs have machines with as many as six reels showing. You can imagine (or maybe you can't) what the odds are on hitting such a machine. They're high enough to keep any half - sane person far away.

If anyone advises you that they can foretell just when a jackpot is due to drop walk away from them, fast. Not even the mechanic who repairs the machine can possibly foresee what is going to show in that little glass window.

There is a law of averages (and I bring this up only because of later chapters in this book) that says on a three reel machine the jackpot will hit on an average of once in eight thousand plays. However, this doesn't mean that you can watch someone play the machine seven thousand nine hundred and ninety-nine times and "know" that on the next play — play number eight thousand—the jackpot will come through for you. The law of averages simply states that the jackpot drops *on the average* of once every eight thousand plays. You *might* hit it with your first nickle or dime. You *might* stand there for a week, pumping money in as fast as you can, and never hit it.

I must add two things, just in case you might ever get any cute ideas about using foreign coins, or slugs, or tampering with a machine in any other way. In the State of Nevada, you can draw down a stiff fine, or jail term —or both—for this sort of action. And all casinos pay a goodly chunk of dough out weekly to employees who watch for just such attempts!

Incidentally, to show the average mentality of the slot machine player, approximately five million dollars is lost every year, in Las Vegas alone, by players who hit a jackpot and *don't know it!*

Most slot machines in Vegas state in plain English on the front "Three bars in ANY position PAYS a Jackpot."

Most players fail to read this or, reading it, fail to understand. They think that the bars must be straight across, in one line, to constitute a jackpot hit. In most clubs the payoff is automatic in such an event. That is to say the machine dumps the money. But, if you can read you'll know that one line above, and one line below, if you have *three bars in sight,* no matter what their position, you have hit a jackpot. All you have to do is call for a change girl to collect your money, because the jackpot does *not* drop automatically in this event. But the poor suckers, either unable to understand what they've read, or ashamed to show their confusion and call over a house employee to explain the bit, simply drop another coin in the slot, pull the handle, and having erased the jackpot, resume their play.

I contend that anyone playing a slot machine, hour after hour, day after day, should not be embarrassed to display his ignorance because if he weren't ignorant, he wouldn't be there in the first place!

The strangest part of all this to me is that you can stand and watch a player spend fifty dollars, hit a ten dollar jackpot, have a free drink on the house, then go to the restroom, come out, and pump his ten bucks right back into the same machine. He'll leave the premises, happy and grinning, with the remark, "Oh, well, I didn't expect to win anyway. Just came down to pass some time away, and I figured I'd spend about fifty dollars."

You'd be surprised how many people make that or similar remarks, and not only around the slots, but also at the craps table or the twenty-one table or the roulette wheel.

So, to you people who come to Nevada with the avowed purpose of losing fifty or a hundred dollars I say, on behalf of all the operators in the State, "Welcome, brother. Come again, and come often—as often as you can." We have a saying in Las Vegas that goes like this; "Show me a happy loser, and I'll show you an idiot!"

When you realize that somewhere between seventy-five and eighty percent of the income in downtown Vegas comes from the slot machines, you have to begin to realize how many honest-to-God suckers there are in this world!

Other "sucker" games, which call for no thinking, are the Big 6-wheel and Chuck-a-Luck. Of course, as will be explained in later chapters, I think an American has the right to spend his money any way he sees fit; to buy a house or a car he can't afford, to take on payments for a full-length mink coat for his wife on a take-home check of seventy-five bucks a week, or to pay seven and a half for a tough steak and a split of champagne that cost the management a grand total of a dollar and a quarter, for the dubious privilege of watching two or three strippers take their clothes off. It's his money. He earned it. He's entitled to do what he wants to with it, even play slot machines, which at least gives *him* the vicarious thrill of gambling. Actually, playing the slots is not gambling in any true sense of the word. "Contributing" is a far better term for it.

At that, when I think of some of the wild and completely uneducated play I've observed at tables where you *do* have a *chance* to win, I have to agree that some of these people would be better off playing the slot machines anyway.

"Think" is the keyword—the magic word in any form of true gambling. None of the games such as 21 (Blackjack) roulette, craps are nearly so difficult to play as they first appear to be. They are really simple games. However, you'd be surprised at how many people—probably one in ten—sit in on these games, knowing nothing about the rules, knowing nothing about the proper procedure of play, knowing nothing about money management. They belong in the slot machine parlors.

You may say it's fun to gamble, win or lose. Let me tell you, it's a lot more fun to win—or, if you must lose, to lose with the house's money, not with your own.

Chapter II

"COMPULSIVE LOSERS"

It would be a little unfair if I skipped too lightly over one of the more important facets (freaks, if you prefer) of gambling—the so-called "compulsive loser".

Over the years I like to think that I've made a few friends, and perhaps a few enemies, with my complete candor. Some people call it "brutal frankness" in spite of which I continue to take the stand whole heartedly.

Some people shouldn't gamble at all. Ever.

Many people, to tell the truth, are rather *stupid* about gambling, or, as we prefer to call it "gaming". Funny thing though, most people *know* they're stupid about it. They gamble anyway.

Then, there are those, lumped under the same general category, who are exceedingly *brilliant* at certain kinds of gambling, certain games, under certain circumstances, but just as exceedingly *stupid* at others.

For a case in point. An attorney I've known for many years is a top-ranked bridge-player. Bridge is a game which calls for an excellent memory, complete powers of concentration and a mind like an IBM machine, *if* the player is to have the slightest chance at winning. Luck plays but little part in this game. Now this particular man—let's call him "Mike" which, of course, isn't his real name at all—maintains a lovely home and a luxurious suite of law offices in Beverly Hills. He's a bachelor, which helps him some, I suppose. But here's what's really peculiar—Mike is not only a "compulsive loser", but he *knows* he is.

Like we say, those of us in the business of paring a few dollars from your bankroll, "He's a nice guy, but he just can't stand prosperity!"

This compulsion, for which I'm sure the head-shinkers must have a name, doesn't extend to bridge or gin rummy for Mike. At both of them, he is a very tough player indeed.

But Mike is a real sucker for a little game called "Liar's Poker", a game with which you probably are acquainted. But, for the benefit of those of you who aren't, I'll run through the essentials of the game right here.

Got a dollar bill in your pocket? Good for you. Take it out. On the upper right of the face side (George Washington's picture) you'll see the serial number of the bill. This number is repeated on the reverse side of the bill, in the lower left hand corner.

As I write this, I look at a dollar bill I've just taken from my own wallet. The serial number is N-96589271-A.

You'll note that by rearranging these numbers I can reach a 9-high straight. Your opponent, or your opponents (although I advise you seriously to practice this game before you get into it. Plus which I advise you, *never play it with a bartender!*) also has, or have, the same number of letters or digits on his bill, but naturally they'll be different and give him a different hand than yours. You will also note on your buck, that you have a pair of nines. You see, in actuality, you are playing with *sixteen* numbers. Eight of them you're looking at, eight are in your opponent's hand. He, in theory, is in exactly the same situation. He can see *his* eight numbers, but has no idea what *yours* are. Yet, the hand is resolved by any combination from *both* series of numbers.

You don't *have to have* a 10-high straight to call one. You may take the chance that he's holding a "O" in his hand and call that 10-high straight right off the bat. Or, you might call any pair you can think of, waiting for his response to your call. Or, you might call three nines. Remember, *you've* got a pair of them.

This Liar's Poker is unlike other games of chance. It's unlike them because you can call any number of sixes (or another figure) knowing, or maybe just hop-in, that your opponent has about enough to make it—or to go bust.

Then there's another system. It would be to open the bidding with three treys (you have none, do you remember?) If your opponent comes back with four treys, or even three fours, you've got him, *unless* he is actually holding them.

And so the game goes. Until one or the other of you says, "You're a liar", or, as is more common, throws his bill on the table and says "What do you need?".

Don't be fooled by the apparent simplicity of the above explanation. It isn't a simple game. And it gets even rougher as you add more players. With them, it turns into a really tough game, plus which, you may be sure that in a flock of five "sheep" one of them, at least, is really a wolf in a white fur coat!

But let's get back to Mike. Here's a boy who really knows his cards—really knows the odds in gambling. So, what gives with this guy who's played cards (gin and bridge) and, on occasion won, with great players like Jacobi? Yet when he goes up against me in a game of Liar's Poker, he loses.

And not only to me, but to just about everyone with whom he plays this game. Frankly, I'm no great shakes at this particular form of poker, mainly because there are too many imponderables, but I've been so embarrassed playing with Mike, that on more than one occasion I've refused, or at least tried to refuse his money.

I've played him for ten dollars a hand, letting him read his own bill, while I played it "blind". That is to say, I had no bill from which to study, but played with any bill in the joint that I couldn't see.

And, "blind", I've beaten him.

I beat him, not because I'm good but, because Mike has an absolute *compulsion to lose*.

"I feel guilty about winning at anything except bridge

or gin," he's told me, soberly and seriously. "I even went to a psychiatrist about it once. He came up with a great big guilt complex for me but no solution for it. I told him HE was NUTS, and *that* was the end of *that* doctor-patient relationship."

Now here's a guy who handles, in gambling money, about a hundred thousand dollars a year — give or take ten grand. And that's a lot of dough. He's one of the fortunate few who can afford to be a compulsive loser.

But what about the *little* fellow, with the same *big* compulsion? And there are many of them.

I used to watch a big Chinese guy in a joint on Fremont Street in downtown Las Vegas. He was working as delivery boy for a grocery store. He apparently got tipped liberally because every hour, hour and a half, he'd drop into the casino, place anything from a five to a dollar on the 21 table, draw four cards (never more) and — win or lose, walk away, talking angrily to himself.

If he was trying to make enough money at the table to get back to Formosa, or get a relative out of Red China, forget it. He didn't have a chance of making either.

Then, back in the old days, there used to be a shooter who'd bring in a hundred or so to play at the craps table. We used to call him "Mile-a-Minute-Murphy". And, I may add, he was always a sight for sore eyes. He'd edge in at the table, bet the back line and "Don't Come" until he got the dice. Then, no matter how he stood, he shoved every dime of his roll on the line and shot.

If he hit, he'd yell, "It's the luck of the Irish, by

God, boys!", scoop up his winnings and leave. If he missed, he'd shrug his shoulders and walk quietly. I watched him go up against the percentages that way for a couple or more years, and I guess he came up with that war cry only five or six times during them.

Funny thing about it, Murphy was a craps dealer from just down the street, and he knew the odds as well, if not better, than any man walking. He just liked to lose or win in sizeable chunks. He wanted fast action. Needed fast action.

I went to the track with him one day. He picked four of the first five races, got himself together a bundle of about five bills, I'd imagine. Then he went to the feature race, the seventh. Despite my desperate appeals to him, he insisted on putting his whole wad on a long shot, which was eighth out of the gates, ran a dead eighth clear around the track (without a call) and finished twelve lengths behind the *seventh* horse.

"Why?" I asked Murph, "Why would you pick *that* horse in the *feature?"*

If he had an answer, he didn't give it to me. The only thing he knew was that IF that horse had come in, he'd have made a pile of money. A real bundle. About ten or twelve thousand dollars.

And he might not have known it but I knew, he wouldn't have had a penny of it left after two days.

Speaking of "compulsive losers" a professional gambler, who could deal any gambling game ever invented, is my "pigeon" for a game so simple I blush to think about it. It consists simply of each player taking a stack of dimes — say ten dimes each — rattling them and throwing them on the table. One player can take "heads" all the time, or can alternate "heads" and "tails". The twenty dimes hit the table or bar top at the same moment. The player who selected "heads" picks up all the dimes with heads showing, while the player who picked "tails" picks up the others. Now, we'll suppose that one player loses three dimes from the ten with which he started. He now has seven dimes, and the privilege of calling "heads" or "tails". The other player pockets his winnings, and he also uses only seven dimes for the next call. And so on until the game is concluded with one player picking up all the money.

Now, this is the easiest thing in the world to do — to cheat at, if you like. It's all in the way you *pick up your money*.

Pick up your dimes so that they're all stacked "heads" up, in a kind of loose roll in your hand. When you *throw* the dimes, throw them palm UP to get a majority of heads, palm DOWN to get a majority of tails.

It might sound like a magic trick. Believe me, it isn't. It's one of the simplest things I've ever seen. A six-year-old child can master it completely in five or ten minutes. And so can you.

Anyway, this pigeon of mine has a mental block about this particular game. He knows all the tricks, he is skillful at craps, at 21, and at poker. But he simply cannot win at this simplest of all gambling games.

I'd sure call that a losing compulsion, wouldn't you?

I'm reminded of still another man with this compulsion to lose. I knew him at one of the gambling clubs that used to be run hell-for-leather in the old days near Louisville. This guy was stickman for a craps table, an acknowledged master-craftsman. We all called him "Bones", and I never did find out what his last name was. But a stickman in those days ran all kinds of dice in on the unwary. Shapes, miss-outs, taps, everything. And "Bones" was tops at doing it.

He did it by running the substitute dice up and down the side of the stick as he reached for the dice in play. "Bones" practiced his art until he was virtually indetectible. I remember several big crap games when someone working for the house would send out a desperation call for "Bones" to come down and take over as a "bust-out" dealer.

This happened, usually, when the house was losing heavily to some other professional gamblers. "Bones" worked for half the winnings, and eventually, despite a rather expensive way of life, he saved enough money to buy a nice little hotel in Louisville.

I stayed there for awhile, and Bones always loved to sit around the lobby in the evening and play cribbage with me.

Here was a guy so fast on the draw, so fast on the count, that it was almost frightening to watch him operate at a craps table. But at cribbage, I guarantee you I could have trained my dog to best him. At a friendly ten cents a game, which he'd boost to a quarter after his first few losses, he'd drop an average of ten bucks a night to me — before he went out for dinner or he went back to work.

Perhaps the fact that we played an honest game between ourselves might have accounted for this, but I doubt it. It was just, I believe, that he liked to feel that he both won *and* lost at gambling, and his compulsion was to lose a few bucks to anyone in cribbage. It was his means of justifying the methods he used in getting it back with about a thousand percent profit at the craps table.

In fact, just about the only person I've ever met without some form of losing compulsion was the once-famed John Montague. I don't know if you've ever read about John. Many years ago he was the Toast of the West Coast. Most of the old-time pro golfers remember him with more than a little bit of respect. I can, but I will *not* mention names. Names that Montague, armed with only a *rake,* a *shovel* and a *hoe,* beat. Names that belong among the all-time, all-greats in the game of golf.

He was gleefully backed by Bing Crosby and Bob Hope. John never turned pro. There was just too much money in it for him as an amateur — playing against wealthy men. And he shunned publicity like a fish shuns fresh air.

His phenomenal talents didn't stop with golf, however. He received offers to play with at least one highly respected major league ball club, after he'd worked out with them one spring strictly for laughs. He did play a season or two of pro football, but decided the money wasn't worth all the labor involved.

He was a pool shark, a real tough gambler, and was wise to and ran about every type of "con" there was going.

A year and a half ago I ran into John who wanted me to write his life story. I didn't take him up on it, because, interesting as it was, much of it, in my opinion, is best left unreported.

At least, while John's still alive.

Canny, sharp as he was, John had one compulsion: the alcohol. Booze and gambling don't mix, not for any extended period of time, anyway. John got so he would gradually accumulate a bankroll, then he would hole up in a hotel and drink it just about all up, then go out and try for another score.

Recently, perhaps a year ago, John, looking for the bathroom during one of these periodical binges, fell out the window. When he came out of that one, he was paralyzed from the waist down.

So maybe you could say he had a losing compulsion also, no? Even if it didn't show up in his gambling.

Chapter III

"GAMBLING BY THE BOOK"

This is not meant to really be a chapter. It's meant to be more of a warning to you.

From here on out, I'm going to do my level best to teach you how to gamble "by the book." That is, to have the odds more in your favor than you've ever had them in the past.

If you have some method or a system of play that differs greatly from mine, fine. But I challenge you to put it to a test, by trying my recommendations out, and then comparing your winnings.

I don't THINK you'll find my methods better. I KNOW you will. And, it's highly possible that after you've tried my methods of play for a little while, you'll discover some refinements of your own to add to them, making them even more advantageous to you.

For the sake of making my position absolutely clear, I am assuming you *do* gamble. Almost everyone does, you know, in one form or another. In many simple games, such as the matching of pennies, you "know" you're working with even odds. But I know that even then *it isn't always even!*

I am also assuming you'd rather win than lose. And I further assume that *if* you're completely frank and honest with yourself, you'll admit you've been a loser!

You must have been, you know, or you wouldn't have purchased this book in the first place. So, from here on out it's going to be a textbook. And I suggest you read the more important parts several times. Even practice in your own home if you wish. Remember, I can't tell you *what* to do. I can only tell you what you *should* do, and what you *should not* do!

You will forgive me I hope, if from time to time, I drop into this semi-scholarly, dry evaluation of odds and methods of play, a few little anecdotes told and re-told among the pros of the business?

For this, thank you.

Now, read on so that you, too, may be a winner more than a loser. For situations will arise where you *cannot* lose, but once more, remember, they will also arise where you *cannot* win.

And before you hit the tables in the casinos, it's a good thing to know just *what* these situations are and *how* to recognize their inevitability.

We'll begin, in this next section, with the game that offers you the most odds in your favor.

The dice table, or — if you prefer — the craps table.

Chapter IV

"THE 'GALLOPING DOMINOES' "

I said in the preceding chapter the dice, or craps table is where the odds are best for you, the shooter.

The only "luck" you'll find in shooting craps is to be at the right table, at the right time. If the dice are passing even then you must know something of the game before you can begin to take advantage of the "luck" that is there. You must have the knowledge to recognize it for what it is.

Once the dice are passing, the player who knows the game has the house at his mercy. He is betting house money, and all the bosses can do is hope that he sevens out soon. Wishful thinking doesn't help any, because nobody can foretell what's going to happen on the next roll, and the law of averages doesn't seem to work consistently (although it inevitably will come through.)

In other words, you might see the dice miss for hours at a time. You might also see them pass for hours, days, or even weeks.

You can see, now, why there is a rule in all houses for a certain specified "top" on how much money may be rolled by any one shooter on any one shot. For instance, if the dice are hot and passing and some gambler starts playing with house money he figures "what the hell do I have to lose?" He is perfectly willing to press his luck, to let his money lay as long as he can, so that he might be shooting five, ten, or even twenty thousand dollars a roll. Therefore, each table has a sign as to how much you can bet on any one shot. This is called the " House Limit."

The "House Limit" works as a two-way stretch. That is to say the simplest system in the world, which is the old "double up and beat the dealer" school of thought, simply won't work. Figure it out for yourself. Suppose the dice are running neither hot nor cold, but say about average. You go with the shooter for one dollar. He misses. Now you double up and play two dollars with the next shooter. He misses. You now have three dollars invested in the game, so you double up once again and bet four dollars. You miss again. Then it will be eight, sixteen, thirty-two, sixty-four, hundred and twenty-eight, and from there it's only a couple of steps until you reach the house limit. And all of this to get back your first dollar wager!

So, as you see, the House Limit on a game makes

things almost impossible unless the dice are running right. If the dice are running right. that is passing a lot, with each shooter making three or four passes before he craps out, you'd be foolish to fool around with one dollar bets anyway.

Most players are afraid to bet. The dice can be passing but the poor crap shooter is now starting to bet less and less. The average crap shooter feels that dice can't make too many passes and must miss sometime. This makes them (they feel) authorities on dice.

As a matter of honest fact the average guy who goes to Reno or Vegas actually knows very little about the game he is playing; what the actual odds are against his winning, or even understanding, the layout of the craps table.

If you will note the diagram in this chapter you will notice that the numbers are the same on both sides of the table. This is done to accomodate the player, so that he can bet from any position he stands in, because a table can hold up to twenty-five players. At each end of the table there is a dealer to handle the bets. In the center of the table is a man called a stickman. He uses a long, bamboo stick that's bent on the end so that he can rake the dice in after each shot.

Immediately in front of the stickman is a long box in which are what we call the "Propositions." On top of the box is the word SEVEN 5 for 1. This means anytime a player thinks a seven will show on the next roll he gives his money to the stickman and says "Seven." The stickman places the money in the box where it says SEVEN, and on this number the player only receives one roll. If a seven shows the player receives five dollars for every dollar he'd bet, and if it doesn't show, the stickman takes the bet and locks it up.

Underneath the SEVEN are what are called "hard-way-bets"; called the "hard-six," "hard-ten," hard-eight," and "hard-four." The hardway must be made the exact way it is shown on the layout. A hard six is two treys. The player gives the bet to the stickman who places it in the square which shows "hard six." If the six is made another way, such as a four and a two, or a five and an Ace, or if a seven is rolled before the two treys are made, you lose. This applies to all the hard-ways and you receive as many rolls of the dice as are needed to reach a decision.

The hard 6 or 8 pays ten for one. The hard 4 or 10 pays eight for one.

For the novice (or complete beginner) at the game of dice let me add to — or rather simplify — some things which may have crossed your mind. As long as you are standing at the table you are a player, and you may bet at any time you wish. Please do not confuse the word player (as *so many people do*), with the word "shooter."

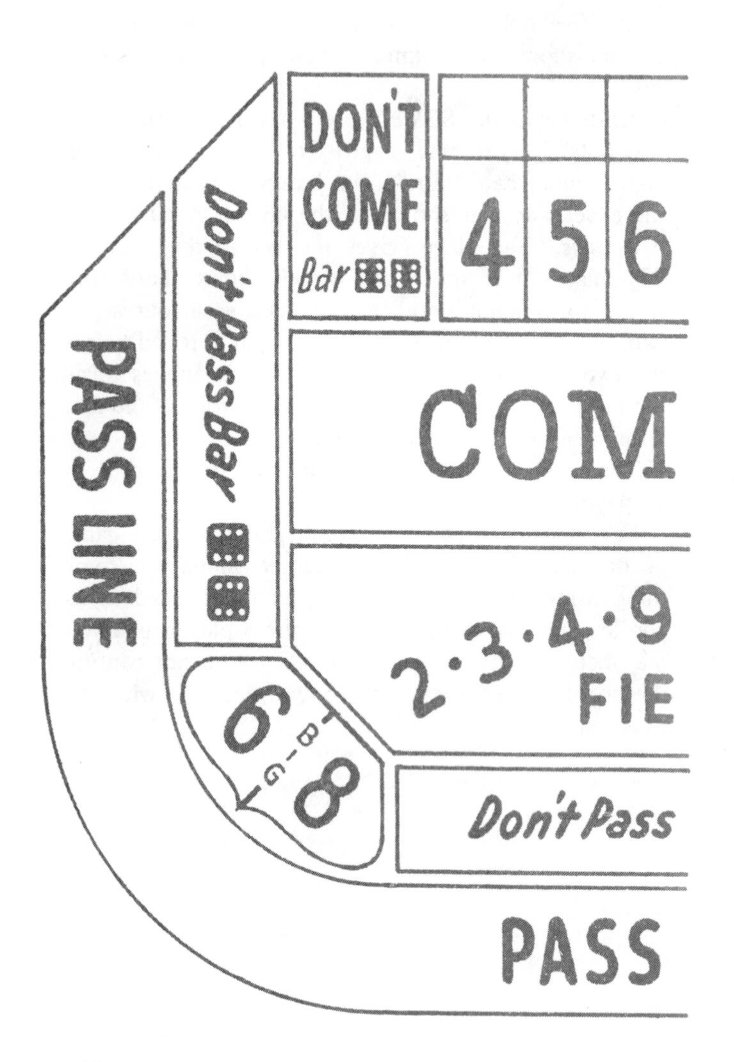
DON'T
COME
Bar
4
5
6
Don't Pass Bar
PASS LINE
COM
2·3·4·9
FIE
6
B G
8
Don't Pass
PASS

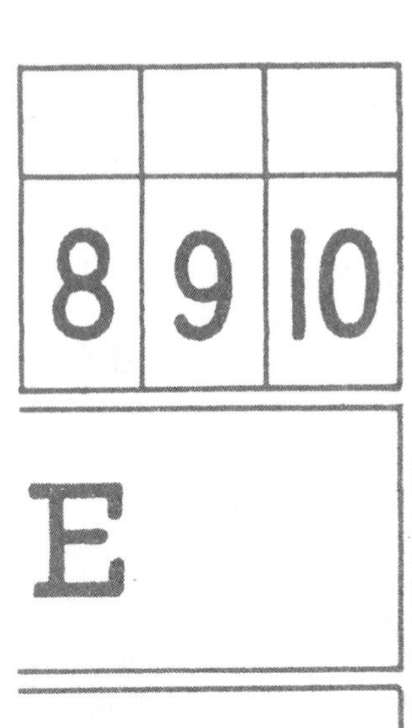
8
9
10
E
·10 ·11 ·12
LD
Bar
LINE
DICE
ANY SEVEN
4 TO 1
HARDWAY
3 TO 1
HARDWAY
7 TO 1
30 TO 1
15 TO 1
30 TO 1
15 TO 1
ANY CRAPS
7 TO 1

Underneath the hard-ways, as you will note from the drawing of the layout, are the numbers of Ace-Deuce, which are three; two Aces, which are two; two Sixes, which are twelve. These are the "crap" numbers, and are one roll numbers. Quite a few players and shooters bet on these crap numbers when they have a good sized bet. This is called "taking insurance" on your money, because if one of these crap numbers should show on the first roll the player or shooter betting that he wins, loses his money. The only catch to this is when you bet one any one of these you must specify *which one* you want.

When betting on Ace-Deuce, the payoff is fifteen for one. On two Aces, the payoff is thirty for one. On two Sixes, thirty for one. You can also make a bet on the Eleven, and you receive only one roll when you wager on eleven showing. The house will pay you fifteen for one if it does. In some clubs you will receive fifteen for one on eleven and three, and thirty to one on the two and twelve.

Underneath the Eleven boxes are the words "ANY CRAPS - 8 for 1." You should remember one thing — when you bet on one of these numbers, and win, your money will ride on that number *unless* and *until* you tell the dealer "all off." Example: say you bet a dollar on hard eight and it shows. The dealer will give you nine dollars and you are still up on the hard eight. But, if you say "all off" or "all down" you receive ten dollars. Many players leave the table after winning one of these bets thinking they have all their money.

One of the biggest money makers for a gambling

house is the player who bets the propositions I have just described. These are the guys who pay the overhead and make the club owners happy. Because they "know their way" around a craps table they figure they're tough gamblers.

It isn't necessary to describe everything on a dice layout, because it's just too confusing for the ordinary player. Refer to the diagram in this chapter when reading about betting the field, big six and eight, pass line, come, don't pass and don't come, and you'll know more about the game of craps than the average guy you see standing up there tossing his chips around like confetti on New Year's Eve.

Again let me impress upon you the fact that there isn't a gambling club in the world that doesn't have the best of it regardless of what game you play. If the percentage wasn't in their favor they couldn't stay in business. The important thing for you to learn is how to make the right bets. This way you won't be eaten up by the house percentage.

It constantly amazes me to learn how many people actually believe they have an even chance to win bucking a gambling house or casino. This would be like a clothing store that sold everything at cost. There has to be a profit or the place wouldn't be there.

For example, if you're a player who likes to bet on big six or big eight (an even money bet) the house percentage is a fraction over nine cents on every dollar you bet. Now if you were to bet me, personally, on the flip of a coin, heads or tails, and we were betting five bucks per flip, but you had to pay me forty-five cents each flip, win or lose, you would soon realize how stupid the bet was. And yet, this is exactly what happens on big six or big eight.

There are plenty of such bad bets to be made on the dice table, and seemingly a never-ending source of players to make them. Where they come from I don't know, and why they seemingly never wise up to the odds against them is another unanswered question in my mind.

Dice is the most popular and exciting game in a gambling casino. It gets the most action, and it's where the big money is won and lost. It is also the best gamble for your money if you know how to bet and how to manage your money.

Also, a crap game is much easier to play than 21. I've seen many people walk up to a crap table, see all the money and chips flying around, all the colors on the layout, shake their heads and walk away in utter confusion, for which you can't really blame them.

Let me tell you this, though, it's much simpler to play, and not nearly so difficult as it appears at first glance. All you need to know about the game is within the covers of this book, plus a little common sense on your own part. A chimpanzee can hit the jackpot on a slot machine, in fact this was an actual occurrence not too long ago. I suppose a chimpanzee could also make ten or twelve passes with a pair of dice, just by mechanically throwing them across the table. However, a chimpanzee could never be taught to protect his investment by managing his money, so that I'll tell you if you can't out-think a chimp stay away from the casinos.

Dice, or craps, seems to me to be essentially a man's

game, although I'm not sure just why. It should be the other way around when you stop and think about it. Women will admit quite frankly they don't know anything about the game and will ask questions on how to play, how they should bet and so on. I admit some of the questions they ask are laughable, but still they're trying.

The smart man will just play and never think of asking questions as it hurts his ego. The only trouble with the ladies is that they forget the answers to their questions, due to the excitement of the game. The gambler likes plenty of action, and that's what you get in a crap game. Any kind of bet, any time you want to, and you don't have to wait a second to lose your money.

In the next chapter I am going to tell you about the only free bet you can make in a gambling casino.

You don't think there is such a thing, do you? Well, this is where you're wrong, and this bet is the one that marks you as a tough gambler to the dealers, the stickman, the pit boss, and the management. This is the bet the house hopes you *never* make.

And this is the bet that can send you home a winner instead of a loser. Now if that doesn't make you want to read the next chapter, you're not a crap shooter at heart, anyway!

Chapter V

"ODDS — AND HOW TO PLAY THEM"

Remember, if the Casino or gambling club could find out some way to get rid of this bet altogether, they'd do it, because a tough crapshooter knows ALL about it. This bet is called the "ODDS."

No dice layout in the world has the word ODDS printed on it and of course no one is going to wise you up to this bet unless you simply demand to know what it's all about. There are thousands and even millions of crapshooters who daily or weekly or monthly participate in the pleasure (?) of the game that never heard of it, and of the few that have and do play the ODDS, only a handful know that the odds are free. There's absolutely NO percentage to the house in it.

Nobody has the best of it, either, either the house or the player. It's the only bet made in a casino whereby the player doesn't give a percentage to the house.

I think the bet will be easier to understand if I first explain about the "pass" or "front" line. When you put your money on this line, you are betting on the shooter to win. Needless to say, you are betting *against* the house. Is that clear so far?

The player places his money on the pass line and the dice are rolled. Let's say the shooter makes the worst possible shot he can without crapping out. Let's say he rolls a 4. Now he must *repeat* that number (in an unlimited number of rolls) in order to win his bet, but — he cannot seven at any time during that sequence or he loses. Four is a difficult point to make when you're shooting, because there are only three ways to make a four, but there are SIX ways to make a seven.

The odds then, are 2 to 1 *against* the player making his four.

These odds are irrefutable, you can't change them. But here is how the ODDS bet works.

Say you are either the shooter or have bet with the shooter. Let's say you've got five dollars riding with him on the PASS line. *You can put any amount of money you wish up to the amount you've bet on the PASS line* behind your bet on the pass line. That means you are taking the odds on the point 4, and if the shooter makes the four, you collect on the PASS line and are paid 2 for 1 for the bet behind.

THAT BET BEHIND, THE "ODDS" BET, IS FREE!

Anytime you can get something for nothing in a

gambling club, take it.

The only time your odds are free is when you have a bet on either the pass line or come. The percentage paid to the house is already paid as soon as you made your bet on the pass line, and as soon as one of these points is made: 4-10-5-9-6-8, you are allowed to take odds free, no charge and a dead-even bet.

This all may sound complicated, but study your layout carefully and you'll see it. The odds on a 5 or a 9 are three to two, as there are six ways to make a 7 and only four ways to make a 5 or 9. Odds on the 6 or 8 are six to five. It's two to one on the 4 or 10.

So, in taking the ODDS bet on the 5 or 9, which are three to two bets, you'd receive a $1.50 back for every dollar you bet. On the Strip, the smallest bet allowed is a dollar, so that if you bet $5 on the abovementioned odds, you'd receive back only $7, instead of the $7.50 due you. You can see that to collect your full odds on some bets, you'd have to bet a minimum of twenty dollars. Ten on the PASS line and ten on the ODDS.

Take the odds, even if it means you drop fifty cents of what you should have received. It mounts up for the club, sure, but your winnings on the odds will pay your room and board too, and as often as not send you away a winner instead of a consistent loser.

As mentioned, the odds on the 6 and 8 are six to five, and of little use to the small $1 and $2 bettor. The key is the five dollar bet. On the odds, the house must pay you six bucks for each five dollar ODDS bet.

Perhaps it doesn't sound like much money to some players, but remember, it costs anyone — big operator or little guy — 9¢ on every dollar placed in action on the board. That's the average. That's the "grind," the "pc" or percentage, for the house, and that's what wears you out in the long run. This runs into a little money for the little player and many times is the difference between a winner and a loser. It isn't what you actually lose at gambling but it's what you save by avoiding foolish bets during a play. By saving, you're lasting longer — and that might be just the time the big hand shows for you.

Remember, you win, when taking the ODDS, eight times more money when a hand should show. Don't wait to hear a dealer or a stickman tell you to take the odds, that this is the time. You'll never live that long, and if they did tell you when, they'd be fired before the shift was over. If you're in doubt as to how much odds you can take on a number, ask the dealer. He'll tell you. Remember, it's your money, and it's a lot easier on your roll when you ask than when you experiment.

Forget all the fancy layouts, the attractive proposition box, crap-out bets, and so on. There's only one way to win at a craps table and I'll tell you right here and now what it is: bet on the pass line and come, TAKING ODDS ON EVERY BET YOU MAKE. If you *don't* take ODDS, you can't win with any amount of money. Also you're not in a position to take advantage of a hand if it should show.

If you're a beginner, or have even been playing *at* the game for awhile, don't try to make as many bets as you can. It will simply confuse you, because, as I've said before, there's a lot of action going on around a craps table.

Bet on the pass line, take the odds, then make one come bet, take the odds. That gives you a pair of bets to watch, and that's plenty for the beginner. Remember, betting a "come" bet is just like betting on the "pass" line, only you are looking for another point.

Now to the finer points.

Here's how an experienced or good player would bet. A bet on the "Pass" line, then two "come" bets, all of them with odds. Now he waits. If the dice are making his numbers, he will now take another come bet, with the odds, ALWAYS with the odds. And so on, if the dice are running right and his numbers are winning, until he has all the numbers filled. As you can easily note, he's no longer playing with his own money, but with the money he's won. In other words, house money. He never makes a new bet until he's won an old one.

How does this work out in actual play? I mean what are the mechanics, involved? Well, I'm no mind reader, so I can't guarantee you what any three numbers in a row will be, but let's make an imaginary situation, not too favorable to the bettor.

Let's say, for the sake of simplification that you're a ten dollar bettor. You bet ten on the "pass" line and the point comes out 4, which is a toughie. You take ten dollar "odds." You now have an investment of twenty dollars on a lousy point. Now you bet $10 on the "come" and the shooter comes out with a 5, which is a little better but not much. The dealer places your come bet on the 5 you give him ten dollars more and say "odds." He'll place your "odds" bet on top of your "come" bet, but so as not to cover it, which signifies "odds." This is called capping the bet. You have two bets, neither of them very good, and you make another come bet and the shooter makes a 6. You give the dealer another ten dollars for "odds" on *that* bet, so that you now have sixty bucks floating on the board.

You wait to see what happens. Your points are 4, 5 and 6.

Something to remember: if the shooter makes the four, you'll get paid, but your odds bets are all off in the "come" boxes when the line point is made. Lots of players will leave the table, not knowing they haven't lost their money. The shooter makes his "line" bet, which was 4. He is now shooting for another number. He makes a seven. This kills all the "come" bets still riding but wait — the dealer will give you back your odds bets, although he'll lock up the "flat" or original bet. So how did you fare on this little expedition?

You bet $60, total. On the 4, which is what the shooter made, you received twenty dollars on the line bet (your ten plus ten from the house) plus your ten bucks on the odds bet, which makes a total of thirty, plus twenty of the house money, because odds are two-to-one on a 4 (remember) which makes a total of fifty, plus your ten dollars each on the 5 and 8 odds, which leave you with a profit of ten bucks on winning only one out of three bets.

No wonder the house doesn't like the "ODDS" and no wonder you should learn more about them!

Sure, you only won $10. "Only." But that's pretty good interest for less than a minute's action, isn't it? What bank pays that good?

Play the game the way it should be played. Don't try to outguess the dice or outfigure the odds. The dice are square hunks of plastic and the odds are automatic.

Remember this: any bum can get lucky, even a chimpanzee. But the consistent, really tough player, is the guy who makes the bet and takes the odds. Take advantage of the dice passing, as it doesn't happen too often and, above all, forget superstitions.

It doesn't do you a bit of good if you walk up to a table where the dice are passing and you don't know how to take advantage of the situation. The world is full of suckers, many of whom have big stories to tell about their last big "hit" in Vegas. That's just before they put the nudge on you for a drink, or a fast finsky 'til payday. If they know so much about gambling, can make that kind of money, why ever come home? Why not stay and become millionaires?

Your big winner doesn't talk about it. He wins. He's usually the quiet guy at the table. He doesn't talk to the dice because he knows they can't hear. He bets the line and takes the odds, and if every table was surrounded by players like him, more casinos than I'd like to think about would go broke in a week. Sometimes there'll be — hell, I guess it happens a thousand times a day — a table where the dice are hot and passing like mad, and yet the house only loses a few hundred bucks because none of the bettors know what the hell they're doing. And the owners sigh with relief when one of the tough gamblers doesn't come in and start that betting the line, come and taking the odds.

Another thing: there are a lot of players who, when

the dice are passing, really passing, start cutting *down* on their bets.

Instead of betting ten or twenty, they'll cut their bets to five, two and right down to one, figuring the dice have got to miss.

Wrong, all wrong. When the dice are passing, *increase* the amount of your wagers. I've seen players leave a game after a big hand, but only with a tenth of what they should have won. I've even seen players stop right in the middle of a big hand and remark: "Well, I got what I came in for" and take off.

Needless to say, the bosses love these players!

Do the dice actually run "hot" or "cold"?

Absolutely. Lady Luck is a strange old girl. There are good days to just stay in bed and read the papers or curl up with a good book. There are other days when you re hitting one table after another winning ten here, fifty there, a thousand more in still another spot.

I know one fellow who won't place a bet at a table where there isn't a good hand running. He covers more territory than an old-fashioned cop walking the beat, but when he plays, and he's by no means a large bettor, he makes money at it, simply because he knows how to bet the line and come bets, and HOW TO PLAY HIS ODDS.

He makes a better-than-average living, and while I have no idea how much money he actually has put away, he's sent a son and daughter through college, owns a nice home and drives a good car. He takes a month's vacation every year, too. Not too tough a life, is it?

There are plenty of regular players, who play almost

365 days out of the year that are tough, too. They set themselves a limit, play the $2 line with a $2 ODDS cover, then go into the "Come" bet, also with the "Odds." That's ALL they play. They'll drop twenty or thirty dollars a day, and when that thirty is gone, so is the player. But playing by the book, as they do, you'll occasionally see them leaving the game a couple of thousand dollars ahead. You can afford to drop a few dollars a day when you play their way!

You see, the "toughest" player that comes into a club isn't the guy who bets it all on one roll of the dice, the house limit, whatever that may be. The casino operators aren't afraid of this type of player. They love him, welcome him. They know he can only win or lose, and in any case can't hurt them. It's the little guy, operating on a short bankroll that gives them fits, especially if he knows the game. The best the house can do is take him for whatever he's got. But if he wins a few grand, he's working with *house* money, and recovering your own money isn't the idea behind a casino!

Chapter VI

"PROGRESSIVE BETTING"

It's a basic concept that if you don't know how to manage your money at anything you can't expect to be successful in any line of business, whether it's making caps, selling newspapers, running a drugstore. This is even more true in the game of craps. A good player who knows how to handle his money well is a mighty tough combination to beat because even if the dice are going against the player, he'll simply hold tight and wait for the passing to start. When this happens, as I've said before, he takes the odds on the number.

Even if there are a couple of these really tough players at a table when the dice start to pass well, the management doesn't worry too awfully much because they know that there are plenty of other people around to throw their money away on all the pretty little boxes, hardways, and propositions, so that they're not really worried.

Many players win half or less of what they should because it seems to be human nature for the player to hoard his meager little winnings and bet less as the dice are passing. These same people, in business, won't even begin to hesitate breaking themselves if a good deal comes along. Yet, if this player stopped to think that when the dice are passing it is a sure investment because everything then is in the shooter's favor, he'd do differently. In other words, when you're playing with the club's money, and if you know anything at all about the game, you'll take advantage of your good fortune.

Unfortunately, most of these same players don't understand or know the gambling business any more than the gambler knows how to make caps, sell newspapers or run a drugstore.

So what do we know? We know that the best bet for a right bettor to make is the pass line and come, always taking the odds. So now, the problem is, how to bet and when to bet. Let's take some of the guesswork out of betting.

To begin with, when you walk up to a crap table and the shooter has a point, don't wait for him to make or miss it before you bet. I've seen many a number show in the "come box" while the shooter will never make the line number. Some players, with little or no experience, will wait, not knowing a bet can be placed on the "come" and will miss out on a possibly good hand. If the shooter has a point he's working on, just bet on the "come." It's another point and you don't have to wait for a decision on the line. But take the odds. Always take the odds.

Now here is how you bet your money and progress as you win. Just keep one thing in mind. You must progress as you win because if you don't you'll be ground out of your money. I would like to say that this is my own theory but I can't do so, anymore than I can say what the odds are on a certain bet. This is the way you must bet if you hope to win consistently. It's called the slow progression method and it calls for considerable caution in managing your money. Leave a little and take a little.

A two-dollar bettor is working at a slight disadvantage because of the house odds, nevertheless, there is still a progression for the two dollar bettor.

$2 on the line and $2 odds. If you lose the first bet, stay at the $2 level. Even if you lose the next five or ten bets, don't change your bet. *Never* bet more when losing. If you should win the first bet, you now bet $4 on the line — $4 odds. The next step is $6 and $6. The next is $10 and $10 — the next is $10 and $10, which will give you a little more money to play with. After you win the second $10 and $10 you bet $15 and $15. This is a high enough limit for the $2 bettor to arrive at.

You will notice that after winning the second bet you are now a winner and cannot lose regardless of what happens after that. For example, you're betting $2 on the pass line and the point is five. You take $2 odds and the shooter makes the five. You now have a total of $9. You now bet $4, the shooter makes a six so you take $5 odds and he makes the six. You have now a total of $20. $19 from the second bet, and $1 left over from the first one. Even if the shooter should miss the next point, you still have $8 left and are therefore $4 winner to the hand. When you're winning, you never decrease your bets. The only time you bet less is after you've lost. This applies to all types of bettors. In other words, you make a bet on the line and lose it. You still make the same amount bet until you win. Now you progress until you lose a bet, then revert to your original bet and keep doing this all the time. Don't get so disgusted that you'll bet more when the dice are missing.

After making a bet on the line and taking the odds you take a come bet which is exactly the same as the pass line bet and works exactly the same way. You progress on your come bet the same way you do on the pass line. Slow progression.

You must have a fair knowledge of the game. Watch, and make your bets without any hesitation or fear. Three bets are enough for the above average player, two for the average player. You can win quite a bit of money at this rate and not be confused as to where your bets are. Also, if at any time a crap shows while betting on the pass or come, make the same bet and continue the same way. Don't let two, three or twelve shake you up. After all, they're on the dice and must show up like any other number.

Here are the progressions for the other group of

bettors:

A $5 bettor starts at $5 — $5, $10 — $10, $15 — $15, $25 — $25, $40 — $40, $40 — $40, $50 — $50. This means half on the pass line and the other half on odds. A $50 limit is sufficient for a $5 bettor and it is applied the same way when betting on the come.

A $10 bettor starts at $10 — $10, $20 — $20, $30 — $30, $50 — $50, $75 — $75, $75 — $75, $100 — $100. He plays the same way when betting on the come.

A $25 player starts at $25 — $25, $50 — $50, $75 — $75, $125 — $125, $125 — $125, $200 — $200. Also, he plays the same way when betting on the come.

A $50 player starts at $50 — $50, $100 — $100, $150 — $150, $150 — $150, $250 — $250, and can either stop at $300 limit or continue up to the limit of $500. He plays the same way when betting on the come.

There is no need for a $100 player today in arriving at a $500 limit. $100 — $100. $200 — $200. $300 — $300, $300 — $300, $500 — $500. He can afford to reach the limit as fast as possible, but he must still give himself a chance to save on the way up.

A note of warning for high players, that is from $100 up. There are quite a few clubs in the State of Nevada that have a very low limit on their games and many a player will get hooked in a small limit so that even if a good hand should show, they're in too deep to get even because the low limit stops them. It doesn't hurt to ask what the limit is before you start to play.

By following the above system, you have been

managing your money, and saving while playing. And, you are now what is called a "tough" player with a good chance of standing right in there with the boys and betting it up, instead of standing on the sidelines watching the hand finally show.

Gambling, it has been said, is a peculiar game — without money you can't play it, but by playing the right way, the way I've outlined above, you are forced to take advantage of dice passing, and after the shooter makes the second pass, you cannot be loser regardless of what happens from then on. If the dice are not making any numbers, you're betting your minimum bet so that you're not chasing your money. The only time you'll be a chaser is when the dice start to pass with the club's money.

I might add that when playing and the dice are running both hot and cold, making a few passes and numbers and then missing out, you're now gaining in money value. As the dice are making three to four passes and a few numbers. Don't be afraid to raise your original bet. You're now at the higher limit. That way you're taking advantage of the dice passing, and getting full value out of the club's money.

Now, if the dice should catch on and start to pass, you're in the driver's seat. And, if they cool off, simply revert back to your original bet.

One thing I might add here. As you know, if you've ever been to Vegas, anything smaller than a five dollar bill doesn't really count as money. Of course, this is a sort of brainwashing you get, because five silver dollars rattling in your pocket simply don't seem to have the same value as a five dollar bill in your wallet.

Nevertheless, if you've had a good day at the tables, don't let the amount of money in front of you scare you. This money is in action and doesn't belong to anyone until a decision is reached. In order for you to be betting any amount of chips you have to win them first. You didn't wish them in, you won them by betting the right way.

Two rules. Bet more when you're winning. Bet less when you're losing. Any other way can be your downfall as it has been for most players. When you're playing the above mentioned method, after the second pass, you cannot lose to the hand. Many players have walked into the middle of a hand and only needed to pull out a twenty dollar bill to win thousands of dollars. You can win three to four thousand dollars by starting to bet $10 — $10, if you should be fortunate enough to walk into the right table, and enough passes — say like ten — are made. This doesn't even count the come numbers. This has been done thousands of times by good crap shooters. It will be done thousands of times more so long as there are players who know how to manage their money, and how to make the best bet for their money so as to take advantage of the dice passing.

Dice is both a simple and complex game of chance. No one can tell you what the dice will do on the next roll. They can guess. I suggest you let someone else do all the guessing. Play this way. Don't go back to your old style of playing where your money doesn't have a chance to do anything for you. Give yourself a chance to enjoy gambling instead of suffering before during and after every roll of the dice. Above all, — ALWAYS TAKE ODDS. They're the only thing you receive for free in a gambling casino.

Chapter VII

"WRONG WAY CORRIGAN'S"

I always call a guy who bets against the shooter (or *WITH* the house) a "Corrigan."

It isn't really a good way to bet, although as often as not some monkey's uncle will come along and do real good at it, which is more than okay with the management, because it encourages other "wrong" bettors, and this is a form of betting in which the house has the distinct edge.

You see, the club has to take some advantage over the "wrong" bettor, otherwise every shooter in the world would be fading. And winning.

All clubs that have crap games "bar" the ace and or sixes, which is the only edge the house has against the wrong bettor, and which is quite enough when you stop to think about it.

In Nevada, the layouts bar the two sixes. This simply means that you, the "wrong" bettor, will just get a standoff if the shooter rolls two sixes (total 12) on his first roll. You don't lose, you just get a standoff. The bet stays there until the shooter rolls again. If the shooter rolls any other craps, you will win, so you see the house's percentage against a "wrong" bettor is a slim one, and at first glance, this would seem like the right and proper way for a smart bettor to operate. In a friendly game at home, this is true.

The minute the shooter comes out with a point, you have a distinct set of odds going for you. Odds are 3 to 2 he won't make a five or nine, 2 to 1 against his making four or ten and 6 to 5 against his making a six or eight.

Now, here's the catch: the club will gladly allow you to call your bet off anytime you want to when betting wrong, and of course many players do so if they think the shooter will make the number.

BUT — when betting wrong, *you must lay the odds.* I can't think of a better example than to have you stand here by my side and watch with me as we keep our eyes on three players. The shooter, the guy who's playing the line and the wrong bettor.

Watch. See, the shooter comes out with a four. The "wrong" bettor has placed, just before the roll of the dice, a ten dollar chip on the "don't pass" (wrong). He apparently doesn't think the shooter can make the 4, so he tosses in another ten, which makes *twenty dollars for which he can only win ten dollars.*

That's correct. Now the "Line" bettor has only $10 going for him, but he can invest his money in the "Odds," which gives him, when you come to think about it, a pretty considerable nudge over the wrong bettor.

Yet, I can name you many a so-called "Top" gambler who will consistently bet on the "wrong way" or "Don't pass" only and exclusively because they have an ingrained belief that the dice simply won't pass as often as they'll miss. They just can't figure everything the "right" bettor has going for him, and that the dice needn't pass worth a damn for the guy who plays the "come" box and carries insurance on his selections by taking the odds.

We have a saying in Vegas: "Most 'wrong' bettors leave town in a fifty thousand dollar car — a Greyhound."

I don't consider that there's anything wrong in betting against the dice. Plenty of players, all humor to the side, have won considerable money betting wrong. There are only a couple of things. The wrong bettor almost HAS to "chase" his money, and then it's "goodbye, Charlie." Also, he has a strong tendency to drag back his bet if the shooter comes out with a 6 or 8 for a point, these being reasonably easy numbers to make. The operators gladly let you drag. Why not? Now you're in the jaws of the old "grind" or "PC," and the house is steadily eating you up, a small chew of nine per cent all the time.

A "wrong" bettor must use the same system as a "right" bettor. He must wager more when winning, less when losing. Also, as a "don't" bettor must lay the odds, he's got to have a little more money to play around with as he must win more bets than he loses, whereas the "right" bettor can make money even when the dice are missing.

This I will state for a positive fact: a man who bases his betting tactics on betting against the shooter will tell you that dice hit less often than they miss. What he fails to understand is that the right bettor will win more than the wrong bettor, much more, in fact, as he gets more for his money and doesn't have to put up so much of it.

But if you *MUST* bet wrong, remember the rule in all gambling: BET MORE WHEN WINNING AND LESS WHEN LOSING. Take advantage of luck, sure, but manage your money at all times. Even a wrong bettor can be a tough bettor. Nick the Greek is a wrong bettor, although I personally doubt very much if he's made a nickel off the dice over the long haul.

I keep wondering where he gets his bankroll. No one seems to know.

There are only four bets, I may add, in closing this chapter on craps, where the player will get the most for his money: Pass line, Come, Don't come, Don't pass.

BASIC RULES OF THE ROAD

Don't — bet propositions.
2. *Don't* — bet big 6 or big 8.
3. *Don't* — bet the Field.
4. *Do* — bet pass line.
5. *Do* — bet on the Come.

6. *Do.* — (if you prefer) bet on the Don't pass.
7. *Do* — (if you prefer) bet on the Don't come.
8. *Always* — Take ODDS on your money.

Above all, stick to these few and simple rules. Don't listen to advice. Don't be afraid to ask questions, but ask them of a dealer or a pit boss. Play the method I've outlined, and you'll win more; and who knows? You might get real hot and wind up a millionaire, screaming and hollering about all the income tax you have to pay Uncle Sam.

There are worse things you could wish on an enemy, right?

Chapter VIII

"LAS VEGAS VIGNETTES"

Stories about gambling, sin and various and sundry other matters pertaining to Las Vegas are heard and read about almost daily and throughout the world. Some of them are true. Some of them are not true.

In a way, I suppose it's all good for Las Vegas, because as the man once said, "Say something good about me if you will, something bad about me if you must, but please don't ignore me."

Did you ever see a whiskey "shot" glass? You know, the kind with the little white band around it — just a little way down from the top? This glass is fairly standard all over the country. A couple of the boys were sitting at the bar in one of the downtown casinos, not too long ago, and had been having a bad night at the tables. During the course of their conversation one asked the bartender for a shot of whiskey, which was poured and placed in front of him. He turned the glass around carefully, picked it up and sipped at it until the whiskey was at exactly the level of the white line, which is about three quarters of an ounce of liquid in a one ounce shot glass.

"I'll bet you five bucks I can put five dollars worth of dimes in this glass without spilling a drop of the whiskey," he told his buddy.

I became interested and moved over to watch the action myself. I have since found out this is an old gimmick but it was new to me at the time. Both the characters were half crocked, so I stuck around to see what developments might arise. The one called over a change girl and got five dollars worth of dimes from her. Then he started sliding them into the whiskey glass, one at a time, very carefully, working all around the edge of the glass. When he finished the whiskey was still in the glass, and by this time three or four other guys had gathered around to watch. "Now," said this guy, "I'll tell you what I'll do. I'll make another little bet with you — with all of you. I can get ten more dimes in that glass if each one of you will lay me six to five. Any takers?"

Everybody got on him and he calmly, with the greatest most delicate actions in the world slid in ten more dimes, picked up his thirty dollars and left. I walked down to the other end of the bar, ordered a shot served the same way, and got myself a fistful of dimes. I wanted to see how many you actually could put in one of those glasses without losing any of the booze. I spilled my first drop after I'd put in seventy-five dimes, so I figured the little guy had a good thing going for him, and sure enough he did. So far as I know, he's still using this particular gaff on the tourists, and during the busy season in Las Vegas goes from bar to bar finding a fellow "loser," and making as much as two and three hundred dollars a night. The sad part of this story is the little guy's not satisfied, and always goes to drop his nightly winnings on 21 or at the craps table. I guess it just goes to show you that none of us is perfect.

Now, that's the story of a screwy bet. Just remember this. If you pull this even once, you've got your money back, plus a nice profit on the purchase price of this book.

Here's another story, also a true one. In 1950 a sailor who was at heart a fairly timid soul, walked into a brand new casino on the Strip, on its opening night, and threw twenty-seven consecutive passes with the dice. You can check these figures, but if he'd had the guts to let his money ride he'd have busted the house and closed it on the same night it had opened, because he would have walked out had there been no limit on the game, with $268,435,456.00. He left with only $750, being, as I said, a timid soul. Nobody, to this day, knows who the sailor was. He vanished like a sinking ship into the desert with his $750.

The odds against making twenty-seven passes are exactly 12,467,890 to 1. The dice are still on display. On a velvet pillow.

There was quite a legend, which you'll still find in

tourist guides, about a certain "Quejo," who was supposed to be the last of the really wild Indians, and who also — supposedly — was responsible for the deaths of a number of people in and around Las Vegas right up until the year 1940 when his body was allegedly found in a cave some few miles to the northeast of the city, along with fossils and a giant sloth and a pair of wooden dice.

Personally, I think that good old Quejo took the rap for a lot of unsolved slayings, but you have to admit he was a mighty handy legend to have floating around for certain elements.

The late Mike Todd, who was once called the greatest showman of our times, reputedly was on his way to the West Coast to try and pick up a bankroll for his next epic. Inevitably, he stopped off in Vegas, and decided to buck the tables. His bankroll consisted of exactly five dollars, but he got on one of those streaks and being a very tough gambler indeed, before daylight arrived was winning somewhere in the neighborhood of $200,000. He asked that the limit be taken off the game, and the bosses obligingly agreed. At dawn's early light, Mike was broke. He met his friends for breakfast and they asked him how he'd done during the night. Todd shrugged philosophically. "I dropped five bucks," he said.

* * *

Here's a little bet that might make you some money someday. Get a group of twenty-five people together and point out the fact to them that in a group of this number the average must be not quite one birthday for each two weeks of the year. You bet them, at even money, that two of them have the same birthday. Ask them to write their birth date down on a piece of paper, then you call the roll and you'll find you have an excellent chance to make $14.00 on every $100.00 in action.

Now, I'll tell you why. The odds are almost exactly 4 to 3. While this is highly favorable, it's no sure thing. You beef up the chances as much as you like by increasing the number of birthdays. You don't have to do this with a large collection of people. You can make such a bet by just opening an edition of Who's Who, anywhere in the book and take the first twenty-five or thirty birthdates you find listed there. You can make this bet if you find the right sucker, even when the number is raised to seventy-five, and at that level, you could only lose one bet in four thousand. They don't come much better than that.

Betting even money when the odds favor you 4 to 3 isn't the silliest pastime in the world. We should do so good in Las Vegas!

* * *

One of my favorite gambling stories concerns gambler Arnold Rothstein. He liked the sudden, big bet. More than this, Rothstein had one ambition. He wanted to win a million dollars on a single horse race.

Now Rothstein owned a stable in his own right, and among the horses was a two-year-old, SIDEREAL. This horse had not won in five starts, but Max Hirsch,

Rothstein's trainer, had been carefully bringing the horse along in secret workouts. On July 4th, 1921, SIDEREAL was entered in the third race at Aqueduct. In cheap company, as he was on this day, and with the odds up because of his past record, SIDEREAL was the perfect tool for yet another Rothstein betting coup.

Trainer Hirsch knew this but hadn't received any word from Rothstein so he assumed SIDEREAL wasn't going to run and left the horse in the barn at Belmont Park six miles away. Two hours before post time Rothstein decided he wanted the horse to go. He knew the horse was sharp, but Rothstein still was at the mercy of normal racing luck, which fact mattered not at all to him.

Rothstein went upstairs to his clubhouse box and sat down, called for one of his men who promptly went out to round up the rest of Arnolds "beards" — people who bet for him — and went to work on the track bookmakers.

SIDEREAL who was thirty to one on the opening line started to drop in a hurry as the biggest betting splurge in racetrack history gathered momentum. This was before the day of the parimutuels, and all betting was done with bookmakers, much as is done today in England. Therefore each bookmaker had his own odds and had to pay off on whatever price was offered when the bet was made. Today, of course, with the electronic system which changes the odds in a flash, such a betting coup would not be possible. With only one hour left, Hirsh went out to the paddock, leaned against the railing, and thought about roads. He could see his horse van getting stuck in the holiday traffic, or an unexpected breakdown, or God only knows what else.

Finally, the betting was done, the horses were saddled up, and Hirsh had less than a minute to produce SIDEREAL when the van pulled up. Rothstein picked up his field glasses, never changing expression as SIDEREAL came from fourth to run head and head with another youngster called ULTIMO, then finally pulled away to win at the wire. Rothstein complained to his wife about the heat, which was the only comment he had to make for the day. He wasn't enthusiastic. He had won $850,000.00 on the race, a record that is still standing. But it wasn't the million Rothstein was shooting for. Instead, Rothstein himself got shot on November 4th, 1928 over a crooked card game. He died two days later.

Speaking of names, I am sure you've all heard of the famous old team of Clayton, Jackson and Durante. When Clayton passed away many years ago it left a big gap in Durante's life that I don't suppose has been filled to this day. Clayton worked as manager for the trio, undeniably had a lot of talent, and was a fair to middling golfer. He associated with a rather weird assortment of characters and because his "day" generally began at cocktail time, Lou regarded daytime as fit only for attending funerals and such.

In the fall of 1930 at the Belleclair Club in Bayside, Long Island, the others in his golf foursome — Titantic Thompson, Frank Costello, and Big Bill Duffy — found this out. Belleclair was noted for being a high stakes course. If you were off your game there, you could lose the family jewels and go in hock for your plus-fours.

Clayton was having an awful time this particular afternoon, being in bad shape after a hard-drinking, hard-working night put in at his Club Durant. On the other hand, the rest of the foursome were in fine shape. Duffy had been up early attending to the business affairs of his bootlegging empire, and working out a couple of phoney matches for his fighter, Primo Carnera.

Costello was clear-eyed, had been busy all day doing whatever it is he has always done for a living.

Thompson, who had discovered a couple of suckers during the breakfast hour felt great.

The three of them were murdering Clayton. Starting on the back nine, Lou took a seven, and it cost him thirty-five hundred dollars to square his losses thus far in the match. But now things started to break for him. Long shadows were criss-crossing the course. He broke even on the fifteenth, and took a deep breath or two. "I may live," he announced. By the seventeenth hole, darkness was coming on fast, and so was Clayton. "Give me a cigarette," he asked. "I think I'm through coughing for the day." He won two side bets on the hole. The eighteenth was a short par three and by this time it was almost completely dark and Clayton was humming. After birdying the hole he was only $2,500 behind. He suggested they play another round, and everyone laughed. You couldn't see anything, it was so dark. "Then, we'll stay right here and play for $1,000 a shot," Lou suggested.

This price was too good to turn down for these high

living, high rolling partners of his, so they accepted his challenge. Clayton arranged for the doorman to park four cars around the green and turn on their headlights. The caddies went ahead and measured the shots. Whoever came closest to the hole with his tee shot would win a pot of $1,000. While Clayton was about a fourteen handicap player, he had everything going for him, and the eighteenth green, bathed in headlights, reminded him of the cafe dance floor. Lou wiped out his $2,500 deficit in less than a half hour. It undoubtedly was one of the great comebacks in golf history, because after an hour he was $1,500 ahead and getting better by the shot.

When the match broke up and Thompson, Costello and Duffy started to grumble, Lou held up his hand. "Listen," he said, "I'm not the kind of a guy to take advantage. I'll give you a shot at me tomorrow."

"Fine," Titantic said. "What time shall we look for you?"

"Nine o'clock at night," Clayton replied. "And it's fine with me if you come a little late. I'll hit a few while I'm waiting!"

Chapter IX

"ROUND AND ROUND SHE GOES"

Many years ago, there used to be a song called "I'm the man who broke the bank at Monte Carlo." It was from some hit Broadway musical or another. The name of the show is beyond my recall, but I remember just about cracking up with laughter the first time I heard it. Now, there are four so-called "Standard" gambles in which the player stands a chance to make a winning due to both luck and skill. The other so-called "gambling" games involve no skill whatsoever, and can be played as easily and with as much chance of winning by a six-year-old as by a mature, experienced, thinking adult. In other words, there's no skill required to play and win or lose at Keno, the Slots or any other games set up along similar lines. The odds are so overwhelmingly in favor of the house that you'll get ground out in a hurry, without a chance of using your wits, because there's only one way to play. The odds are set firmly. You can't switch bets or evolve a system. When the house odds are great enough, even the laws of chance are removed from the gamble.

Of the four "standard" types of gambling, Roulette is perhaps the least attractive. It looks much simpler than it really is. Can you beat a roulette wheel? I say "yes." Now, there are many stories told about roulette, and it's true that you can both win and lose sizeable amounts of hard-earned loot at the wheel.

First, the odds are made to look very attractive. Second, around a crowded wheel someone hits a winner almost every time and in fact this is almost inevitable, so you're standing there right beside the people who are winning money, and you feel like a member of the group. Maybe on the next roll of the wheel you'll be the lucky winner.

Now, in order to learn how to win at roulette, you must first know *exactly* what the best bets are. This isn't too easy to explain. There are more "sure-fire systems" to beat roulette, most of them dreamed up by people who will simply sit, watch and make notes on the frequency of certain numbers hitting over a protracted period of time. Almost all these theories revert back to the old "double up and beat the dealer" thing, which is about the surest way I know to spend your evenings trying to hitch hike a ride out of town.

Like all gambling games, you bet MORE when you're winning, LESS when you're not. That seems like a simple first rule to me, regardless of what kind of game you like to play, but I'm still shaking my head when I watch the suckers (there's no other name for them) who, the minute they get ahead, start cutting down on their meager winnings. The complete story of all games is "in for a little, in for a lot." The trick is to know the difference between a "little" and a "lot," and when to get "in."

There are right ways to bet roulette, and there are wrong ways to bet roulette. For instance, I know of one man who comes in and plays nothing but silver dollars on the red. He'll play for hours at a time, and whenever he wins, he lets his money ride. When he loses, he goes back to betting a dollar again, always on the red, nothing else. At first glance, or to the novice, this seems like a good bet. It follows my basic precept of "bet big when you're winning, small when you're losing," so where's the contradiction?

In the first place, this is a lousy bet to begin with. You have no way to protect yourself on such a bet, and in addition to the black cutting into a 50% "against" you, there's the house nudge, the "0" and "00," which are green, and which won't pay our aforementioned friend a penny. I admit that with any luck, you could pick either "red" or "black," and win a little or lose a little. I've seen red turn up fifty times running, believe it or not, and I'll add this: there were two guys at the table that evening. They made about ten bucks apiece out of the whole entire deal, because they just couldn't bring themselves to believe that the red could show so many times. They'd win a few times, then switch to black, or aimlessly strew chips all over the table with their "winnings." As I've said so many times, you have no "winnings" or "losses," at any game until you walk away from it. Money in action doesn't belong to either the player or the house until a decision is reached, and it's always *your* decision.

So I watched these two guys play, if you care to call it that, and I almost broke up. They'd play red, win, let their money ride, win again, let their money ride. Now they'd step back from the next spin of the wheel and consult with each other. Won on the first hit, $1, so he now has two bucks riding, his own dollar and the dollar winning. Won on the second hit, $4, third hit $8, fourth hit, $16, fifth hit $32, leaving him $31 clear profit, and NO black has shown yet. Instead, a Red came up while he was debating what to do. That made six Reds in a row, so he switches to Black. Lost, $1. Doubles his bet again, Lost $3.

And so it went. All of which leads up to my telling you repeatedly: NEVER get off a winning hand, a winning streak. No matter what game you're playing, be it roulette or what, stay with the winners. If you're betting black or red, odd or even, stay with what you're winning on. Don't change in the middle of a run because you get a "feeling" that your luck's about to change.

If you're nervous, take a walk, light a cigarette, have a drink at the bar, then come back and start fresh, but DON'T QUIT ON A WINNING PROPOSITION.

Tip: the girls simply love to play roulette, and do, on the average, just about as well as the men, because they simply scatter chips around. It averages out. There are many kinds of bettors: "hunch" bettors, those who play the first two numbers of their telephone, their age, anything. You've got to see it to believe it.

I said a little earlier in this chapter that there is a certain amount of true skill involved in the game of roulette, and I realize this can easily be misunderstood by the reader. The skill involved is simply in the knowledge of where, when, and how to place your bets. Once the wheel starts turning, and the little ball starts rolling, all anyone can do is wish it into the right number and color, just as you'd "wish" a long downhill putt into the cup when playing golf.

Getting back to the system players, they quite naturally think they have a better chance at betting the simple bets. If you'll look closely at the layout, you'll see that betting on the red and black or odd and even numbers to show, or one to eighteen to show, or nineteen to thirty-six are all "even-money" bets. They are simple enough to make, but the house is against you because there are thirty-eight numbers on a roulette wheel — one to thirty-six — and the single and double zeros.

Some players have worked out a mystic type of system which calls for betting on both red and black at the same time, only betting more on one than the other after a certain number of turns. This, on the surface, is a stupid way to bet. As you must lose one of your bets, regardless of what happens, and if either the green zero, or double zero shows, you lose both of your bets. Yet, believe *it* or not, there are not only people in Las Vegas who offer to "sell" this system. There are also people who are obtuse enough to purchase it.

Once in awhile the word will get out that a wheel is off balance (which is almost impossible). Each roulette wheel is checked once or twice daily, and there's frequently a big rush to the rumored off-balance wheel, with everyone trying to get down on the same two or three numbers. I suspect that many times these rumors are deliberately started by the casino operators themselves because a wheel would have to be so far off balance it couldn't even turn before the ball would drop into one particular section. Why? Because the wheel turns one way while the little ball spins the other.

Contrary to popular belief, roulette does not have to be an expensive game to play, and it does offer a pleasant form of relaxation. For example, on the Strip in Vegas which by and large maintains a higher minimum wager on all its games than the downtown casinos, the smallest chip you can play is for ten cents, and you must buy only a minimum of $2.00 worth — or twenty chips. Of course, you can go upward if you want to play for higher stakes, by playing 25¢ chips, at $5.00 a stack. In downtown Vegas, you can buy chips for $1.00 a stack. There are twenty chips in a stack and the bets are paid off in stacks of twenties.

A roulette wheel and layout is really something to see, as the chips are all differently colored (not according to price, but so that the dealer can speedily and easily tell who the winner may be). Then, you've got red, white, green and black on the wheel and layout.

There are more women players, strangely, than men, possibly because it's such a very colorful game.

But, round and round the little ball goes, and where it drops, nobody knows.

All I know is, the house starts with a basic 5 and 5/19ths percent against the player. Of course, the house odds are considerably better (for the house) when action moves into the field of numbers.

In my next chapter I will tell you exactly how to play roulette, and what I consider to be the best "method" (please note I don't use the word "system").

Chapter X

"HOW TO PLAY"

I think it will help you if you refer to the layout in these pages from time to time, as I try to explain the game to you.

In looking at the layout, please note that every number is squared off in a box, including the zero and the double zero. Unlike any other game of gambling, the lines that separate the numbers can all mean a different price payoff. If you bet a number straight up you must put your chip directly on the number. If it hits, it will pay you thirty-five to one. If you wish to bet two numbers next to each other, you can place a chip on the white line between them, such as ten and eleven which are next to each other. But, the odds are a little less this time. You receive seventeen to one.

If you want to bet three numbers with one chip, you place a chip on the white line like ten-eleven-twelve, and this chip must be placed on the line where the ten begins. Any of those three numbers hit, your odds go down again. You receive eleven to one.

If you wanted to bet on four numbers with one chip, say twenty-two, twenty-three, twenty-five and twenty-six, you place the chip directly in the middle of where those four numbers meet each other. Any one of these four numbers hit, once again the odds go down. Now you receive only eight to one.

If you want to bet on six numbers with one chip, say sixteen, seventeen, eighteen, nineteen, twenty, and twenty-one, you place your chip between the sixteen and nineteen, on the outside, or end line. Payoff on a hit for this is five to one for every chip you bet.

Underneath the bottom numbers of the layout, you will note three empty squares. These are called columns. If you place a chip in one of these, and any number in that column hits, you receive two to one for each chip you've bet.

There's another bet made on the layout, in which you receive six to one for every chip bet. This is the zero — double zero — one — two — three. To make this bet, put your chip on the outside line between the single zero and one.

Outside of the layout you will see the numbers, first twelve, second twelve and third twelve. Place your chip in any one of these boxes and if the numbers come up that you've selected, you are paid two to one. This is sometimes called betting the "dozens."

On the extreme outside of the layout are the even money bets. From left to right they read, one to eighteen, even, red, black, nineteen to thirty-six, and odd. If you bet one chip on one of these and you win, you receive one chip back.

Anytime you make a bet and win, you are paid off, but the dealer lets the original bet stay down. If you don't think it will hit again, you must remove the bet yourself. Many players have walked away leaving their original bets behind because they weren't aware of this fact. This is not an attempt on the part of the house to cheat you out of your money, but simply to help speed up the game.

Now, most good wheel players follow a system, or method, as I prefer to call it, of play, which is unrelated to the layout itself. They will bet what is called a section of numbers. Five in a row, that are next to each other in the wheelhead that spins around, such as seventeen — thirty-two — twenty — seven — eleven, so that if the ball should drop into one of these numbers and "jump" or bounce out, it might fall into a number next to it, but in the same section. This is about the best method of play I can recommend.

Most clubs have limits on their wheels, only on individual numbers. The limits vary, so if you have any intentions of playing for the higher stakes, it's best to find out what the limits are before you sit down and start playing.

The toughest wheel players are the section players who will walk in, buy twenty silver dollars, and play their five numbers with $4.00 on each number straight up. If one of those numbers hits, he'll spread all of his money on the same five numbers. Then, if another one of these numbers hits, the club's in trouble. Say there's a twenty-five dollar limit per number. He bets twenty-five dollars on the same five numbers, and does it again and again, as long as he keeps on hitting. When he starts to lose, he walks out. All he can possibly lose is his original stake of $20.00, but he can win the joint if his numbers should happen to show.

This is what I call a tough player, and the owners and operators of the casinos know most of the regulars who fit into this category. They all hope that the guy is going to have a bad first roll on the wheel. Needless to add, they're always happy to see him leave.

Of course, every gambling game has a way of being beaten — illegally. If the dealer is having a real busy session he has the chance to pick his head up only when the ball drops. It takes a pair of crooks to pull this gimmick. One will stand at the head of the wheel, with the few chips he bought at the cashier's window,

ROULETTE

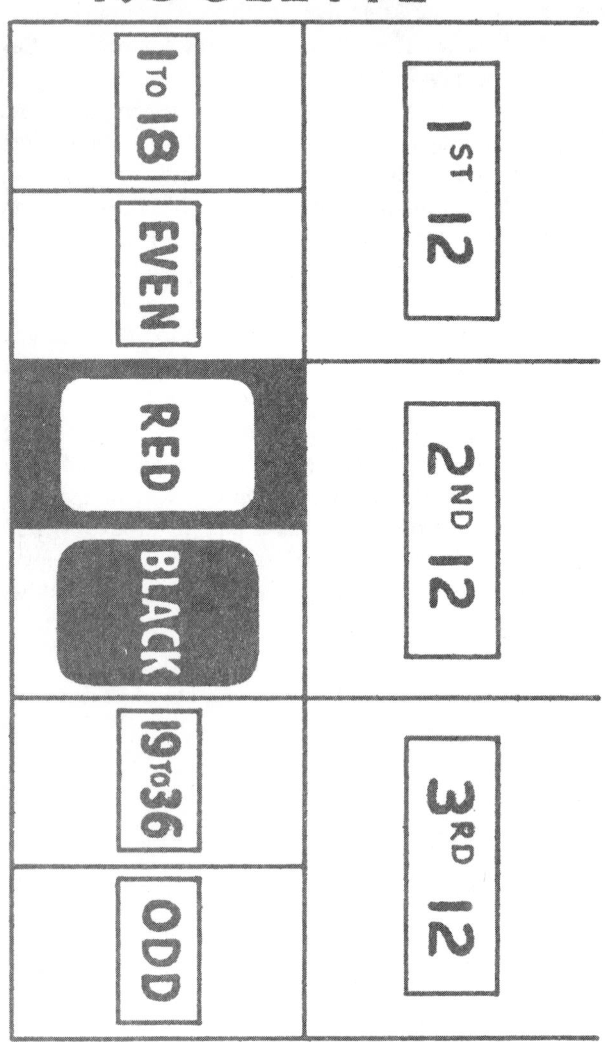

0-00 AREAS GREEN

0
00
1
2
3
4
5
6
7
8
9
10
11
12
13
14
15
16
17
18
19
20
21
22
23
24
25
26
27
28
29
30
31
32
33
34
35
36
2 TO 1
2 TO 1
2 TO 1

looking as though he is going to play. Crook number Two, stands at the other end of the wheel, where you'll find the high numbers. When the ball drops, the dealer must turn his head to look at the number into which the ball fell, and if it should drop into one of the high numbers, the dealer's had it. The cheater near the high number (who, incidentally, could give a professional magician lessons) will move a five, or twenty-five dollar chip underneath a wheel chip on the number. These crooks train themselves to both see the ball drop and move at the identical time. Now the crook that placed the chip under the wheel chip will walk away as soon as he's done so. When the dealer starts to pay off on the number, he finds a five or twenty-five dollar chip on the bottom, and the cheater standing at the head of the wheel politely tells him, "That's mine." And who is to say it isn't?

Now what does the house do about all this? In the first place, a player standing at the head of the wheel couldn't place a bet at the other end without having knocked somebody down to get there, so the dealer, knowing he's been caught napping, pays off, and bars the player from the game. What does the crook care? He's just made $935.00, and if he can get away with this once or twice a week, he's earning a pretty fair living.

Of course, in Vegas, and in Reno, as well as Tahoe, there's a very close network among the houses and casinos. A description of these crooks is circulated immediately, that is if the dealer can remember what they looked like. Still, there are a great many roulette wheels in the State of Nevada, and these characters continue to get away with their game from time to time, although today most clubs compel the dealer to place the five and twenty-five dollar chips on top of the other chips whenever a stranger is at their wheel. If a five or twenty-five dollar chip is found underneath when a number is hit, and the dealer doesn't know the player, the player doesn't get paid.

There is another way to illegally beat a wheel, but it isn't tried too often, as when you buy wheel chips they can be cashed in only at the wheel, and are of no value anywhere else in the casino. They can't be traded for money or house chips at the cashiers cage. You must buy your wheel chips from the wheel, and cash them in at the wheel.

Now, as most roulette layouts are near the frontdoor, a common practice used to be for a cheater to bet in big chips, a couple of hundred dollars in the last "dozen" which pays two to one. If the ball drops in the last "dozen" the crook just stands there like a natural man and politely waits for his payoff. If it doesn't fall into that last "dozen" the crook will grab his money off the layout and run like a bandit for the front door. This is now largely overcome in most clubs by the dealer who lets the ball roll around a couple of times, reaches down, picks up the money the crook has bet, replaces it with a wheel chip, and says "This is a one hundred dollar chip." As I said earlier, the wheel chip is worthless except at the wheel, and the crook, if he grabs it and runs has only gotten himself a worthless souvenir.

As I've said before, your best chance to beat the wheel is to bet the numbers but not spread your chips all around. The more numbers you bet, the less chance you have.

The tough wheel player will bet five numbers straight up, preferably from a wheel section. If you're operating on a short bankroll — rather than spreading all your winnings back, if you should hit — hold back a few dollars and get to where you're playing with the house's money, rather than your own. Just as soon as possible. Then, you can really go crazy (and drive the house crazy at the same time!) if that section starts to hit.

Always bet more when you're winning. Go back to your original bet if you start losing.

A word of friendly advice here: Anytime you make a big hit at roulette, get up and walk away. The chances for two big hits in a row are practically none. That is to say, if you win four times running, out of the five numbers you've been playing, you've got enough money to go see the show in the cabaret, have a good dinner, and go to bed knowing you have a few thousand bucks to play with tomorrow.

And, remember this also. One lucky streak won't make a professional out of you. It's a long step from betting 25¢ chips to $25 chips, and you need a lot of mental readjustment to get into the upper bracket gambling class.

Chapter XI

"ODDS (AND ODDBALLS) AND ENDS"

I was once asked by a nationally-distributed magazine, of some popularity, to write an article on "How to Have Fun in Las Vegas on $50."

It reminded me of an acquaintance of mine, a bachelor, whose only responsibility is getting out of bed when the alarm goes off and getting to work on time.

My advice to him was the same I'm going to pass along to you, so let's start at the beginning. He had a system.

Not a gambling system, but a "have a good time for fifty bucks" system. I may add that he'd picked up considerable knowledge the hard way before we ever got around to discussing the matter, and I'm sure he's picked up some more since that time.

Naturally, being a young, lusty buck, he was interested in "where the girls are."

Prostitution is one thing that isn't legal in Las Vegas. It ran wide open in the old days, when they were building Boulder (then Hoover) Dam, in the notorious and wide open "Block 16," which many an old-timer will recall with mixed emotions. They operated on the same identical principle as the infamous "Cribs" of many of the river towns. The girls parked on their steps or chairs, outside, clad in only the flimsiest of underwear, and believe me, you could hear some pretty wild propositions in those days. There was no "strip" in those days, that land then belonging to the horned toad, occasional gila monster and myriad rattlesnakes. The gals were not permitted to "hustle" on the streets of Vegas, and were allowed downtown until darkness, to do their shopping and gambling and whatever. Any caught on the street after dark were hustled down to the train station and shipped in any direction they wanted to go, with instructions not to come back.

But I digress.

Certainly, there are ladies in Las Vegas whose favors aren't too awfully difficult to come by, but my friend, the bachelor, wasn't interested in professionals. And had he been, he probably couldn't have afforded it, as the going price starts at about fifty bucks, so there would go his whole entire bankroll at one fell swoop.

Later, he found that Main Street (which is the real name of the "strip") was the best hunting grounds for single girls, unattached divorcees and the like, but his big problem was "how to make the scene on the strip with a short bankroll?."

Gradually, he evolved the following system. He'd drive to Vegas every second week-end, taking only fifty dollars in his pocket. The rest of his scratch he left in the bank in a "special" checking account. He'd even leave that checkbook at home so that no temptation might befall him. He hit the city limits, and drove immediately to the service station, where he gassed up for his return trip, placed a five spot in an envelope, signed the envelope and left it at the station.

You'd be surprised how many people do this, by the way. Now, presumably, he had something like forty dollars left. And plenty of time to get rid of it or make it grow. As he generally drove to Vegas at night, he'd arrive early in the morning, and eat a hearty breakfast, drink several cups of coffee, light a cigarette and stroll around Fremont Street until one of the spots looked as if it might be having a little action. He'd drop in and get ten silver dollars, and hit the crap table. Then he'd move over to the twenty-one game, seeing how he'd do there. If that was no good, he'd go to the bar, have a couple of beers, then get five bucks worth of change and play the slots. By nightfall, following this system, he was generally broke. No point in hanging around, so he'd get his car, go back to the service station, get his finsky, and take off for L.A.

He'd been doing this for some time when I met him, and I asked him if he'd ever had a lucky day.

"Oh, yes," he said, "I hit a hundred dollar jackpot one time, went out to the Strip and had a good dinner, watched a good show, and even shot some craps for five bucks a throw."

I started to question him. Surely a man who'd played 21 or shot craps 26 times a year had to get lucky, if nothing else, once or twice, just by the law of averages. He shocked hell out of me when he started displaying his ignorance of the games. He knew literally nothing about either of them. He'd come to the conclusion that you couldn't win with a forty-dollar bankroll. Seems he'd been playing 21, trying to make the number on every hand dealt him, and that he was taking all the long and foolish bets on the craps table. He figured that, with a short bankroll, you'd better get down on the longshots that pay better odds.

Well, to make this little story a bit shorter, I took the time to thoroughly indoctrinate him in how and when to place a bet, when to "hit" and when to "Stay" in 21.

"Maybe," I told him, "you won't win by this method the first time out, but you follow it, and I guarantee you'll have a hell of a lot more winning nights than you've been having."

He's living proof of the fact that when there's only one correct way to bet, when there is a method superior to all others, that's the one to follow. Never mind if the guy on your right at the craps table just hit a big eight or six, and you miss coming out. You're playing the correct method and he isn't. He got lucky, but you follow him around for the rest of the evening and I guarantee you that a guy who doesn't know how to bet will lose his roll before morning.

Anyway, my friend does better, a great deal better. In a way, I guess I'm responsible for his becoming known as a rough, tough player — for that's the reputation he's got in Vegas. He even knows a lot of girls there!

* * *

Incidentally, before I get on to another story, I must tell you this: the guy I was just discussing, the guy who wanted me to write a piece on how to have fun in Vegas for $50, didn't like the article I wrote and, in fact rejected it.

"We're not trying to educate America on how to gamble and win," he told me when he called me to say he couldn't use the article. "But you can do *something* besides gamble in Vegas and have fun, can't you?"

"Well," I felt compelled to tell him, "you can watch a good floor show. Have a good meal. Then drive back home. And if you don't want to gamble, why in the hell go to Vegas in the first place? After all, Vegas isn't a mill town. The only other excuse I could think of you going there would be if the Air Force transferred you to the base outside of town!"

* * *

I've heard a great many people say, like they were standing on soap boxes in bughouse square, that the reason salaries for "name" entertainment are so high in Las Vegas is because all show people are heavy, compulsive gamblers.

In a sense, that part about their gambling instinct is well-thought-out. What these orators don't realize, however, is that most of the same jokers they're discussing have business or personal managers, who make all arrangements for dates, contractual agreements, and so on. And that most of those high-salaried entertainers are on what you might call a weekly allowance of spending money. Their managers invest their money for them in rental properties, real estate, take over the car payments, house payments, even the grocery bills and bar tabs. Some money they invest in municipal non-taxable bonds, and some money they just sock away in a trust fund to be paid over in the form of a monthly allowance when the entertainer chooses to retire.

So while a guy may be making fifteen or twenty thousand dollars a week in salary, the bosses of the casinos are very reluctant to give him any credit at the gambling tables. Legally, gambling debts are uncollectable, although the casino operators collect most of them, one way or another, for they take a very dim view indeed of someone who runs up five or ten thousand dollars in gambling debts and then blows town.

As for the show people, in eight cases out of ten, the casino makes out his or her paycheck to the star's business manager. The star may actually be drawing three hundred bucks a week.

There are exceptions, as I have noted. One is Joe E. Lewis, who can ask for and get just about any salary he wants, because it's almost a dead cinch he'll leave town with less than he arrived.

Joe is really a tough gambler, if you want to know the truth, but either his drinking befuddles him so that he gets careless, or if he has hunches so strong he can't resist betting them to the hilt, I don't know. I've seen him walk away a big winner, many times, but it just seems as if he can't stay ahead.

Incidentally, there's a rumor around that Joe's on the wagon. If this is true, liquor stocks will take a sharp tumble on the stock market. Most people scoff at the whole thing and said "if he's sober, how does he do his act?"

Personally, all I know is that when he hollers "Post-time" during his act, and finishes the drink he has in his hand, it isn't Coca-Cola he's tossing away. It's straight booze.

And he's a great star. And when he says his famous line: "The horses I follow follow the other horses," it's almost a way of life with him. Joe doesn't give a damn, anyway. After he was knifed, and left for dead during the gangster years in Chicago when rival hoodlum-owned clubs were bidding for his services, Joe figures he's been living on borrowed time.

Strangely, I might add this: it isn't generally nor widely known, but Joe is a generous contributor to churches and just about any organization for kids. He's also a soft touch for old-timers he knew many years ago. On the outside, Joe is a warm, lovable clown, having a ball. Inside, I'm not so sure. I think that within that ultra-sophisticated shell hides a man who humbly thanks God he's still alive, and who prays for an opportunity to help his fellowman. End of speech, down off soapbox.

* * *

Few people realize that England is an easier place to get down on a bet than any other nation in the world. In 1961, a most liberal Betting & Gaming Act went into effect. That same year, Britons gambled away some $3 BILLION dollars, approximately 62% of their 1961 budget for defense. Movie theatres and dance halls, hard-hit by television, have been changed almost overnight into bigtime bingo parlors and slots, or as the British call them "Fruit" machines have blossomed forth in many unlikely locations. A headline in the *Daily Mail* blasted: "LOOK OUT, MONTE CARLO — MAKE WAY FOR LONDON."

Chemin de Fer, not unlike our game of 21, is all the rage among the royalty and well-heeled tradesmen. It's limited to two players, who alternate as banker. Each gets dealt two cards and may draw a third, with the object of getting as close to 9 as possible. Tens and picture cards count zero. Ten days after the largest of the new *Chemin de Fer* or as the British call them "Chemmy" parlors opened, someone slipped a biblical encomium on its manager, blond and beefy Tim Holland, now 37 years old: "He hath filled the hungry with good things; and the rich he hath sent empty away."

* * *

Here's a little philosophical note: the tough gambler, who bets his minimum when the cards or the dice aren't falling his way, as compared to the "scared" gambler, who increases the size of his bets as his money dwindles, is somewhat like one guy betting on the climate and another on the temperature. The Tough gambler knows that while it might be hot today and cold tomorrow, he only has to wait for the average climate to roll around and he's still in business. The "scared" bettor who chases his money, can be wiped out by a cold snap. He's shooting for the whole works at once.

* * *

Columnist Sheilah Graham reported that Sandra Dee, the perpetual teen-ager, blew $40,000 over the tables during an engagement at a plush casino by hubby Bobby Darin. Darin, reported the columnist, refused to pay any part of it, at about which point they split up.

"All those high salaries paid to performers in Las Vegas," continued Sheilah, "usually get back to the house via the tables — and I do mean Donald O'Connor's and Phil Silvers'."

Eddie Fisher reportedly blew a big chunk during his last stay in Vegas. If he did, he could afford it. "Ben Casey," the dour-faced TV "doctor," whose real name is, of course Vince Edwards, was reported to have dropped $20,000 at a single session at the Desert Inn. Even Walter Winchell suggested that Edwards' best bet was to stay in Hollywood and continue grinding out a more than adequate income in television. Vince also likes to play the ponies, and this of course reminds me of one of my favorite funnymen (now deceased, God rest his soul), Joe Frisco.

Joe was a gentle man, although not always a gentleman, if you know what I mean. He became famous years and years ago for his derby, cigar and cane and stuttering monologue. I'd known Joe, prior to his death, for many, many years. He was also a good friend of author John McPartland (also deceased — my God, where's everyone going, anyway?).

In the early days of TV, Joe made somewhat of a "comeback" with his famous horseplayer bit, and was hysterically funny to anyone who'd ever been in a bookie shop. Joe, I would estimate, had been in at least eighty-five per cent of them. In fact, not too long before his death he made what I considered then and still consider to be an epic in the comedy field, but as few of the present-day generation had ever heard of or seen Joe, Capital Records had some doubts as to its initial sales.

"Hell," Joe assured them, "if ev-ev-evry Ggggguh-damned b-b-bookie b-b-buys a c-c-copy, we'll s-s-sell over a m-m-m-million!"

The record's feature side was called "Mother's

Tears," and if anyone reading this has a spare copy, please send it to me, care of this publishing firm. I'd love to have it.

Toward the latter years and months of his life, Joe was constantly borrowing money. None of us who lent it to him ever expected to see it again, nor did we, but it was never a big bite at a time; what was so funny about the whole thing was that Joe thought so much about horses, he borrowed at track odds. He never hit you for a five-spot or a ten, or even a deuce to get himself something to eat. It was always:

"Hey, Ja-Jack, l-l-let me t-t-t-take f-f-f-ffour-forty until t-t-t-tomorrow."

Or two-twenty or eight-eighty.

One of his closest friends was Marion Davies, retired motion picture star, who owned the first big hotel in Palm Springs, The Desert Inn. Marion drove to Hollywood at fairly frequent intervals and whenever possible, allowed Joe the use of her shiny black Cadillac complete with chauffeur.

One night, along about midnight, John McPartland and I were walking down Vine Street, not too far from the Brown Derby, neither of us feeling any pain, if you know what I mean, and along came Frisco on the other side of the street. He rolled down the window on his side of the car and hollered something at us, then imperiously ordered the chauffeur to make a completely illegal U-turn. Joe stuck his head out the window of the Cadillac and asked, earnestly, in his stuttering voice, if either of us could let him take eighty-eighty until tomorrow.

"I g-g-g-gotta s-s-s-show some c-c-class," he explained. "This j-j-j-joker's been driving me all over t-t-town and I want to give him a nice t-t-t-tip."

McPartland, who loved Joe, said, loud and clear (and John had been a former drill sergeant) "I don't mind a mooch, but I'll be G-g-g-g-godamned if I'm g-g-g-going to give my b-b-bread to a *mechanized* mooch!"

John was so made he'd picked up Joe's stutter. I was prostrate on the sidewalk howling with glee as Joe regally waved his driver to move along. "M-m-m-must be a couple of n-n-nuts," he remarked airily. "B-b-b-boy, I don't know w-w-what this t-t-t-town's coming to since they invented t-t-t-television!"

As long as we close on this note, I'll start the next chapter on "how to beat the horses." It can be done, you know, and is being done every day by *smart* horseplayers.

Chapter XII

"HORSES, HORSES, HORSES!"

Back during my salad years when vaudeville was still all the rage, we used to go to the theatre, watch a newsreel, a Harry Langdon comedy, a Mae Busch and John Gilbert feature film. Then would come the thrilling moment when the strains of the mighty Wurlitzer were heard. The organ would rise on hydraulic lifts (playing the last few bars of the closing theme of the feature) and a spotlight would fall on the organist, a guy like Bill Dalton or Jesse Crawford, who were not only great organists but also great personality boys.

They'd play a number "by popular request," then the projectionist would throw slides on the screen and you "sang along" with the organist, who would stop at the end of the first chorus, swing around on his stool, flash a pearly-toothed smile, and hold up his hand modestly to stop the modest sprinkling of applause. We all waited with bated breath because, you see, we KNEW what was going to happen next.

"I thought that was *pretty* good," he'd announce, and we'd all chuckle in anticipation, "but I just *know* you can do better than that. Let's have the ladies, only, sing one chorus. Ready?"

So the females (who generally outnumbered the males two to one at the matinees) would really give out, leaving it up to us guys to take the next chorus. I must say it was fun, and then Bill or Jesse would start some walloping, hell-for-leather number like "The Fifth Hungarian Dance" or "Stout-Hearted Men," and as the mighty Wurlitzer sank into the pit amidst roars and whistles and applause, the whole pit band, sometimes as many as sixty musicians with a most energetic director came up on hydraulic lifts, carrying right on with the same number, fully orchestrated. After a delightful fifteen minute interlude of live, not recorded music, during the course of which the orchestra leader, also a showman in his own right, would turn between numbers and make some remark that would convulse the audience with laughter. Then, playing a get-off number, the pit band slowly sank to below-footlight level, and came to a crashing halt. Then, the play-on music for the first act out of eight live acts would start, the stage lighting would change sharply, the curtains would part, and we had a sensational, delicious and somehow magic hour of solid, *live* entertainment. TV, phooey. I'm convinced that if someone could recreate that scene in the theatres today (and they did as many as four and five shows a day!) and charge the same prices (matinees, 75¢ for boxes and loges, 60¢ for orchestra and 35¢ for balcony seats), they'd play to land-office business.

Now what has all this nostalgia to do with horses and betting on horses? For one thing, about every second or third week there would appear on the theatre bill in this vaudeville house I mentioned, and in similar houses throughout the country, a young lady dressed in what was then considered a daringly revealing ring-master's costume, complete with whip, and two guys dressed in the guise of a horse. In later years I found out that the girl was merely window dressing for the act, and as she was inevitably quite attractive frequently was replaced during the course of the long season, because of the better offers she received, or a blossoming romance. The two guys, however, inside the horse outfit never changed, and were, in fact, highly trained and extremely skilled dancers and athletes. Their movements were perfectly coordinated and strangely enough, the guy playing the rear end of the equine had the toughest part of it all, as he worked "blind," depending entirely upon his partner to lead him in all the right directions. Everytime the horse would "rear," or sit down in a chair, the back half took the beating and did all the work.

I mention this because during the years that I plunged heavily on the ponies I often felt like the back half of the above mentioned team, and if that isn't the hard way of getting into a chapter on horses and horse betting, I challenge you to come up with a tougher one!

I still wince when, at infrequent intervals, such an act shows up on the Ed Sullivan show, or some other variety program, partly I suppose because of my sympathy for that poor, sweating wretch playing the rear end, and there may be quite a little self-identification involved in my reaction as well.

I say that because during my horse playing years I walked like a horse player, talked like a horse player, and even acted like a horse player — or at least what a horse player was popularly supposed to act like. I think I have played about every system in the book with little success, as in the first place you're dealing with a pack of ten or twelve enormous beasts which are by and large a fairly stupid animal, and which have only one thing in common with any other animal in the world. This consists of a leg on each corner.

While it is true that some horses will run a better race at a certain distance, it is not true that the horse "prefers" this distance each time out as so many of the handicappers claim. A horse prefers one thing. To eat, sleep, and loaf as much as possible.

Jim Murray, a very astute and extremely funny featured sports columnist, is of the firm conviction that certain horses perform best when certain jockeys are up, regardless of weight, distance, or track conditions, and he adds that the horse runs better for these jockeys because all they want to do is get back to their stable as quickly as possible, preferably before said jockey beats them to dogfood.

I'm not going to mention these jockeys by name, although each has a fanatical cult of followers who will bet any horse ridden by one or another of this group of batsmen.

I played the jockey system far too long to be taken in by it ever again. In fact, I don't even advise betting on the horses because by the time the State gets its chunk of the handle, it's costing you seventeen cents out of every dollar you bet — even if you win, plus admission to the track, plus a few drinks and a sandwich between races, plus a scratch sheet and a racing form and the program and the parking fees. Also, if you like to sit down, you still have to spend a few bucks for seats.

I tell you the truth. We not only couldn't get away with this sort of thing in Las Vegas, but when we made a noble effort to do so (just a few years back) it went over like a brass balloon! The true gamblers stayed away in droves, and the tourists had more fun playing 21, craps, even the slot machines, paying nothing for the somewhat dubious privilege of losing their money in the air conditioned premises and enjoying free drinks and sandwiches.

Who is to say they were wrong? Not me, certainly. However, there is a system, or method, of betting on the horses which, while in no way guaranteeing you'll leave the track a big winner (or even a winner for that matter) will at least give you a better chance to make a few bucks consistently and which is a better method of playing than any one I've ever heard of. Hold your breath, because in the next chapter I'm going to reveal this secret to you.

Chapter XIII

"YOU, TOO, CAN BEAT THE HORSES"

I strongly suspect that the title for this particular chapter is the title of a book, written by someone at sometime. Before I started writing this, I walked down to the book store and the newsstand.

Amazing!

There must be fifteen or twenty books on how to win at racing, sure-fire systems, fool proof, practically guaranteed. Note that word "practically." As I've said before, racing is one of the larger sports in which people invest and lose their money.

The odds against winning are so much against you that there cannot be a sure-fire way of beating the races — unless, perhaps, you own every horse in the race, which I am sure would be severely frowned upon by the Board of Racing Commissioners.

I even leafed through a couple of those books I mentioned, and, honest to God, by the time you'd finish one you'd need the astuteness of an IBM machine plus the naivety of a 5-year-old child to make anything out of them.

Most of these so-called "expert" books are apparently written by guys who operate like the old-time tout. If this doesn't work, try this. And if that doesn't work, here's another sure-fire panacea for all your troubles at the track.

Well, in my book, the only IBM machine at the track is the tote board, and believe me, it doesn't tell half the story.

Probably the most famous of all fraternities is the "If Ida Club," and most of us horse players, past and present, belong to it.

"If I'd of only bet that long shot in the second, I'd of taken home over a grand for the daily double. And the funny thing is, I was *gonna* bet him, only some guy in front of me in the line bought ten tickets on Number 11. I figured he must of known something."

One guy will figure that if a horse bobs his head up and down as he passes in the post parade, he's sure to be a winner, no matter what the horse's past performance, track record or anything else is. Needless to say, he comes home broke, most of the time.

Last year, a filly was running with a so-so record, but she carried my wife's maiden name. I bet her five across the board five different times, and she lost for me, never even getting a call. The sixth time out, my wife wanted to know if I was going to bet her. I looked at the morning line in the paper, saw that she'd been stepped UP in class, and said "Hell, no. I'd rather take the money and get drunk."

Result? My wife "sent out" two bucks to the track (she's a real plunger) and the filly won handily, going away, and payed $98.60, and that's life for you.

Reminds me of a story about Joe Frisco, God love him. Some owner took a fancy to Joe, and Joe strutted proudly around for days telling all the guys that he knew just exactly when this owner's horse was going to win.

Wise guys that we were, and having been "turned on" by this "owner" jazz more than once, we waited for Joe's downfall. Finally he came bursting into the joint one day, borrowing money right and left until he had a sizeable bankroll.

"T-t-t-oday's the D-d-d-day!" he exclaimed, and caught a bus for Hollywood park. The horse won, too. Joe paid off all his creditors, and told them that, out of sheer gratitude that he'd let them know the next time the horse was "ready."

After four or five such episodes, each time this horse winning, mind you, Joe managed to get us all enthused. Next day was to be another big one. There must have been twenty of us in the small caravan that went out to Hollywood Park. We decided to bet ninety bucks each on this horse, as he did indeed seem like a real live piece of action.

So each of us (Frisco excepted) bought three ten dollar win tickets, three ten dollar place tickets and three ten dollar show tickets. Joe sneered at our oettifogging penuriousness, bought ten $10 win tickets, and promised each of us we'd be sorry we didn't follow his example.

The horse ran second, so we each made a nice little profit on our investment, all except poor Joe. "A d-d-d-dog," Joe screamed. "A real, honest to G-g-g-god *dog!*"

That was Frisco for you. He disliked, in fact refused to sit beside or in front or behind a woman at the track. He considered them bad luck and out of place.

Strange things happen at a race track. A friend of mine who bets a lot with the bookies went out to beautiful Hollywood Park one day, and came back so disgusted he never went to a track again, to the best of my knowledge. He'd picked a sleeper, that went off for about sixty to one, and it broke from the gate, took a commanding lead in a six furlong race and held that lead. He was on his way to the cashier's window when he heard a shout go up from the crowd. His "sleeper" had dropped dead, apparently of a heart attack, about ten jumps from the finish line! Talk about running dead last, huh?

To show you what sort of odds are going against you at the track, here's something a friend of mine worked out in round figures (actually low figures, if you want the truth).

You bet $100 on the first race and the track takes fifteen percent of that, which leaves you $85 for the second race. The track gets $12.75, so you now have just $72.25, and so forth through eight (now nine) races. All this plus food, admission, parking, drinks, a Racing Form and seats. If you don't lose a cent on the horses, according to his theory, you still lose $100 for the afternoon's entertainment.

This is oversimplification of course, but uncomfortably close to the truth.

Who's to know? Jimmy Durante was on a kick one day, wouldn't play anything but horses that had red in the stable silks. He won seven out of eight races!

I thank the good Lord that this book isn't being written for the big bettor, although my fondest hope is that someday you'll be able to drop me a line and say "Old buddy, that book was the best investment I ever made in my life." It takes nothing but intestinal fortitude and steel-like nerves to bet a big chunk of money on a horse. More horse players have ulcers than horses. In fact, I've never known a horse to worry enough to get ulcers. There's the track, the starting gates fly open and he runs as fast as he can (theoretically, at least) for the determined distance, and win, place or show, is taken back to the paddock and the "cooling" ring, after which he is given a good bath by the swipe and a satisfying dinner of oats and clean straw to wallow in. Some life, hey?

Many gamblers claim their only thrill at a track is to bet more than they can really afford to lose. They also say that when they gamble for really big money, they're a lot more careful and selective.

Big gamblers also have another worry. They depress the odds with a sizeable bet. Also another ulcer-maker is that Uncle Sam, in the form of your friendly neighborhood tax collector is right there looking at your I.D. card if you win more than six hundred bucks.

And the paperwork that the average horseplayer

carries around with him (see next page) is often as not more weight than the horse is carrying.

Horse racing induces more people to stop gambling — and then to take it up again — than any other form of gambling in the world. You can hear a lot of guys swear off forever, which is a pretty long time, but next to booze or cigarettes, I can't think of a single habit that's harder to quit.

RACE ENTRIES AT TANFORAN

(Clear, fast; first post 1:15 p.m., PDT)

FIRST—Mile and one-sixteenth, 3-year-olds up, purse $2,000.

Sera C. 103 Cashed Out
Fair Mae 114 Blue Sol
Repast 109 No C
Clever Captain 11
Cursee
Stephens

Racing Daily Form

n Boy 113
Fire Duster 110
furlongs, maiden 2-year-old claiming, purse $2,000.
Please 115 Wonderous 115
Sister Slugger 110 Clown Princess 11
Lady Poona 110 Misty Brown
Royal Looking 110 Blank Verse
Christy's Honor 115 Jeannies Gypsy
Aunt Emma 115 Dainty K.
Red Pantaletts 115 Wiggly Tail
I'm Quick 115 Rare Vamp

FOURTH—Mile and 70 yar claiming, purse $2,000.
Gracious Moon 111 Thoug
Bobby's Star 106 His l
Bobby Jr. 109 Bri
Count Trip 114 N

FIFTH furlongs, 3-year-olds, claiming
112 Connie's Chico 115
112 Teddy's Idol 112
15 Oopsie 112
15 Travel Torch 112
7 Lucky's Fault 110
Shadowscribe 115

2-year-old fillies, 2,500.
Dependable 114 Royal Vanity 109
109 Solid Faith 114
Yenoh Ber 114 Goyala 114

SEVENTH—Six furlongs, 3-year-olds up, claiming, purse $2,500.
Golden Mel 115 Mr. Tollgate 107
Mercy Me 112 Prosperous 108
I Step 113 Gramps 115
Glooming 115 Corianton 115
Copy 115

TH—Six furlongs, 3-year-old fillies and mares, allowances, purse $3,000.
120 Savail 115
113 Seems a Queen 117
120 Comeflywithme 108

yards, 3-year-olds

RAC

FIRST—Six
ins, purse
Don Lere
Travel
Capt. C

FOUR
olds, purse

CONSENSUS

HOLLYWOOD HARNESS

1—Lucille Wise, 13; Demon Raider, 11; Meadow Gaines, 8.
2—Rusty Farvel, 8; Coast Commander, 7; Ottawa's Mary Ann, 7.
3—Jim Fay, 16; Dade County Boy, 10; King Darnley, 7.
4—Clark Express, 14; Best Man, 14; Anastacia Tass, 7.
5—Yankee Music, 10; Silver Scotch, 10; Record Mat, 7.
6—Shafter Hanover, 14; Northernaire, 11; D's Doll, 6.
7—Mighty Indian, 19; Eblis Key, 12; Carolina Rodney, 7.
8—Thor Hanover, 17; Leader Pick, 14; Mr. Budlong, 11.
9—Counselor, 17; Quick Jo, 15; Senator Prim, 4.
Best Bet—MIGHTY INDIAN (7th)

TANFORAN

FIRST—
Blue Sol 15
No Guns 11
Stephens Acres 7

SECOND—
Like Well 13
Liberty Pike 11
Gee Gee Em 7

THIRD—
Sister Slugger 13
Clown Princess 10
Misty Brown 10

FOURTH—
Bobby's Star 15
Thoughtful Me 10
His Laugh 8

FIFTH—
Grain O' Sand 17
Running Tears 10
Lucky's Fault 8

SIXTH—
Goyala 22
Sugar Test 8
Miss Dependable 8

SEVENTH—
Golden Mel 15
Gramps 12
Corianton 8

EIGHTH—
Never More 13
Kee 11
Savail 9

NINTH—
Cohoolin 13
Social Steel 10
Jack Outlaw 6

Best bet—GOYALA (6th)

AQUEDUCT

FIRST—
Cindy's Rule 22
Bee Berger 11
Tenama 4

SECOND—
Fr'dom Fighter 12
Excl'sive D'sign 8
Happy Punny 8

THIRD—
Royal Chit Chat 20
Refresher C'rse 8
Dear Ruler 4

FOURTH—
Pointy Park 24
Pleasure Bound 12
Vindent De Paul 12

FIFTH—
Tuscarora
The Sport
Barnaby's Bluff

SIXTH—
Ev'b'dy But Me 17
Sunsenned 10
You Look Cute 6

SEVENTH—
Sunrise County 22
Western Warrior 9
Marlin Bay 7

EIGHTH—
Ole Johnny 16
Adam Henry 10
Taut Ship

NINTH—
Macbrather 25
Follow Thru 9
Tapisvale 8

Best bet—MACBRATHER (9th)

Let me steer you straight about one thing. I know many people who faithfully follow a so-called "ace" handicapper who run columns in the daily papers. I've never known such a handicapper to have a winning season. Bet $2 a day on their selections, every day, and at the end of a year you will be a loser.

There's a difference between the true gambler and the true amateur. The amateurs work out a lengthy soul searching, than ask the first person they meet, even if he knows nothing about horse-racing, for *his* opinion on the pick. The pro makes up his mind and refuses to change it, except for drastic or unforseen reasons.

Now we get to horse "systems," and some of them are so downright laughable it's pitiful. First out of the box is the old "Pyramid" system. Start with a bankroll of $256, and start betting favorites. $2, then $4, the $8, 16, 32, 64, 128, 256. Anytime you win, says the sage who thought this one up, go back to your original $2 bet. On favorites, yet!

You might even last out a whole day at the track, and maybe have your entry fee for the next day, although that's doubtful!

Now, I'll give you some good tips on when and when not to bet horses.

Don't play horses that haven't run for a good while, no matter what rumors you may have heard about "secret workouts." Sometimes they'll win, oftener they won't.

Don't bet maidens or 2-year-olds. They're eccentric and uncertain.

If a horse hasn't finished 1-2-3 in his recent races

and is running against one or more who have, beware.

Don't play when track conditions change too suddenly.

Stay away from show bets as a rule. They just don't pay enough for your investment in the long run.

When a really good horse has a big overlay (much bigger odds than the morning line would indicate) take a shot at it.

The winningest jockey of 'em all, Johnny Longden, believes that the jockey is responsible for about forty per cent of the win, the horse, of course, representing the other sixty per cent. "A good jock," Johnny says, "can get a good ride out of a middle-class horse."

Incidentally, although so far as I know there's no rule against it, (if you're not riding in it), John never bets on a race. "I'm on the track, doing my gambling for a percentage of my winnings," he'll tell you, "and that's a gamble for me."

Longden's advice to the average bettor is to keep an eye on a good horse and wait for him to be set down in class. "That's win time," Johnny claims. "If you keep your eyes on a couple of good horses who are right up there *with* the leaders, watch for *them* to step down in class, that's when they'll win."

Here's a tip for you fans who like to bet jockeys. Longden, like many another jockey, gets his mount from his agent, but unlike lots of other jockeys, refuses to accept a mount he doesn't care to ride. And the reason he doesn't care to ride a certain mount, as the general rule, is because he thinks the horse is just plain out-classed.

Now here is the word you've been waiting for: a

winning system that almost *always* sends you home a winner! But like so many other things, you must have a bankroll. Your bankroll should preferably be $5,000 and this will net you about $750 a week, so a couple or three of you plungers can get together and make some bread. Look it over and see if you can find any holes in it:

1st: Use the $2 bet as a base wager.

2nd: put $2 on ALL horses paying 9 to 1 or better to both win and place. If you lose, you increase the bet $4 in the second race and if you lose again to $5, then $6 then $7, etc. (It's considered smart to stop with a tops of $7). When you win you revert to the $2 bet again.

3rd: If you have winning horses but still lose money on the race (Because you can often win on a horse that pays less than your original bet) you drop your bets one notch. In other words, you have a winning horse for $5 and a $5 place bet, but don't make money. Your next race, your bets will drop to $4 win and $4 place on your horses.

4th: Use common sense. Don't bet races where you have to bet too many horses. Six in a 9 or 10-horse race is too many, for instance.

5th: Don't play trotters.

6th: Why does this system win? Favorites are always overplayed by the crowd, which means that long shots and many a horse that would be "chalk" under ordinary conditions are tended to be overlooked. In the win and place spot you'll get your share of the money like clockwork. If one or two days in a row you don't, the progression of betting is not fast enough to wipe you out or even to damage you seriously. There's never been a combination of losses big enough to nick a five-grand bankroll when this system is used.

Now!

Don't take my word for this! Buy the Racing Form and the newspapers. Don't even go NEAR the track. Let this system work on paper for a month before you give it a whirl! DON'T BET CASH UNTIL YOU'RE SATISFIED IT WORKS!

But if you play it, *play this system without adding any gimmicks of your own!*

And above all, use your common sense. You may find you won't care to play a race with more than nine or ten horses in it. And while I like big purse races best of all because Saturday or holiday crowds always bet the favorite, thus giving you lush odds on the rest of the field, you may not like such races. Don't bet them.

Use this system as a good substantial base.

Above all as a final note of caution: DON'T ADD A POST POSITION "GIMMICK," A "JOCKEY GIMMICK" OR A "TRACK CONDITION" GIMMICK.

It won't do a thing, it can't help and can only hurt.

So racing fans, there's your secret way to beat the races.

Will it work all the time, every time? I frankly don't know. I've checked it in the newspapers from time to time and it always seems to work.

But then I don't have much guts.

I got guts enough to ask you to send me just ten per

cent of your first week's winnings if you DO try it and it works for you. It's the best system I've ever heard of, and it's designed for the benefit of the player, not the tote-board and the state "dip" into the bettor's dollar. Lot's of luck!

Chapter XIV

"GAMBLING — A WAY OF LIFE"

In all of recorded history, we read of gambling, just as we know that man has always eaten, defecated, fornicated, and *profited by every natural human action.*

Things have simply become more complicated as the years and centuries pass and society becomes more or less "reorganized."

It's a matter of record, and you can't evade it, that if a human being wants to gamble, he'll find a way to gamble. If he wants a drink, he'll get one. Bootlegging was a big-time enterprise, for example in Oklahoma up until a few years ago when the good folk of that state decided to discontinue their long - established practice of "voting dry but drinking wet." Now it's legal, so that gangsterism has largely been eliminated from Oklahoma.

I'll point out that there are some pretty stupid laws governing gambling and drinking in certain states, counties and cities where "local option" is exercised. In California, as a handy example, gambling (poker, anyway) is perfectly legal in one section of Greater Los Angeles, and poker parlors have large neon signs. In other parts of this sprawling metropolis, the police can bust your door down and arrest you for indulging in a friendly poker game or even rummy or casino, haul you off to jail, mug you, run a make on you and then arraign you on charges of gambling.

However, and here's a laugh, bridge players can't be busted for playing for money, as bridge has been locally designated as a game of pure skill. Of course, in the stern but somewhat myopic eyes of the law in Los Angeles, the fact that the very first element of bridge is *how to best bet the cards that fall to you by pure luck* means nothing at all. Yet, this same is exactly true of any other card game ever devised by the human mind.

Another laugh: the largest daily newspaper west of Chicago presents what it chooses to call an "impartial" view of the situation on gambling, takes up three and sometimes four of its pages daily with handicappers, entries, past performances of most of the major tracks in the country. This can be sold on the street corner by small boys or delivered to your doorstep. *But let a vice cop catch you marking your choices for the day in this same newspaper* before you go to the track and you're busted for gambling, suspicion of bookmaking.

Or, go in business for yourself. You can run an ad in this same newspaper offering your scratch sheet, selections and expert handicapping service (one of the biggest sucker traps ever devised) but if you decide to handicap your horses and mimeograph a little sheet to sell in cocktail lounges — bang, you're under arrest!

You figure it out. I can't.

Does gambling, legalized gambling, bring hoodlums into the area?

Speaking from a purely personal viewpoint I say "yes." Certainly, wherever the attraction of easy money is to be found, you'll find a number of undesirables. But with a strict Gaming Enforcement Board, the worst of these elements can be knocked out of the box, as we've proved time and again, no matter what the newspaper publicity says, right here in Vegas. Why?

Because gaming or gambling, whichever you prefer to call it, when legalized comes under the control of the state, and is run wide open. Additionally, it becomes like the bar business, which I'm sure you can understand as a comparison. You pay so *much* for a license, fixtures, etc., that it just doesn't pay to have felons (anyone who has ever been incarcerated or convicted for a felony) among the owners, employees or hangers-on. You've got too much at stake to lose, and after all, when the customer can go right across the street and make the same bet and get the same odds, why should he worry about one or more joints being closed down for having undesirables connected with them?

Yet another example of the way things work: in Los

Angeles, if a cop overhears one guy tell another: "If you're going out to the track today, how's about betting a couple of bucks for me on the daily double. Here, here's two dollars and put it on 1 and 8." The moment that money changes hands, the guy who took it can be and often is arrested for illegal bookmaking, the guy who gave it to him is nailed for collusion and if it happens in a bar, the bar might get a suspension. Yet both tracks (Santa Anita and Hollywood Park) are well within the limits of Greater Los Angeles. Figure that one out. You can't sit in a bar and make your selections before the race. That's against the law. You can't even write your numbers down on a sheet of paper, you shouldn't forget them until you get to the track. That's against the law. Needless to say, this law is flaunted and broken almost every day, a thousand times over, but still plenty of arrests are made.

A recent poll conducted by a newspaper columnist reported an almost 70 to 30 vote of "yes" in favoring a state lottery. This would cut taxes considerably. Yet, everytime it's brought up before the state legislature, it's tabled or voted down. Remember, many of these guys make the trip to Reno, Lake Tahoe or Las Vegas regularly too!

I invite you to pay a visit to Las Vegas. You'll see plenty of citizens of the town. They're as well-dressed as the people in your city, and their individual incomes are higher, as a rule. Don't forget that gambling isn't the only business that goes on in a city where gambling is legalized. There are still dairies, bakeries, law offices, insurance companies, fuel oil dealers, electric supply houses, furniture stores, dressmakers, ladie's shops, men's clothing stores, even bag-boys at the supermarkets..

And in Nevada, there's no state income tax!

I predict, from things I've heard and read lately, that it's only a matter of time until California will considerably ease its tax burden upon the average citizen by having a state lottery.

Oh, yes, another thing: if you're caught by the police for selling sweepstake tickets on the Irish Sweeps, you get busted. It's against the law to traffic in these in California. But if you BUY a ticket and win, they put your picture in the paper and you're a big hero (after Uncle Sam gets his cut of your "take"). Figure that out. It's against the law to sell 'em, it's against the law to buy 'em but it's not against the law to collect your winnings. In fact, this same newspaper I'm referring to publishes the entire list of winners, plus the amount they won, which can only encourage more and more of the same thing; yet the newspaper takes a firm stand against legal gambling because "it attracts the hoodlum element."

In my humble opinion, this is a specious argument, but who am I to say so?

My thought would be that *illegal* gambling attracts the hoodlum element. Anyone would rather walk into a legalized horse book (such as we have in Nevada) and place a small wager than to put his money with a bookie in a secret rendezvous. He has TWO worries, the: will his horse win, and if it does, will he ever see the bookie again? Ridiculous. Why not legalize gambling altogether in the state of California?

I shudder to think of what my friends in Nevada

would have to say to this if they knew for sure the real name of the author.

As long as you suckers in other states have to come to Nevada to know the unfettered fun of legalized gambling, it would be downright treason on my part to advocate legalized gambling in other states, especially neighboring states.

We make it easy enough, as it is, I think. For less than Twenty-five bucks, we'll give you a round-trip ticket on a champagne flight, put you up at a nice hotel for the evening, feed you two free drinks and dinner, let you watch a floor show with some of the greatest talent in the world and give you five bucks worth of chips to play with!

Chapter XV

"LEGALIZED GAMBLING"

I'd like to expand on my previous chapter a bit by mentioning exactly what is going on around the U.S. to further this cause, which may or may not be popular, or even patriotic!

It reminds me of the old story about the traveling salesman who got off the train and asked the redcap where there was a poker game to be found in this new (to the salesman) town. He tipped the porter liberally, and the porter decided to level with him as he placed the salesman's sample cases in the taxi.

"There's a game in the rooms over the pool hall," he said, "but I'll tell you the truth. It's a crooked game. The cards are marked and the deck is stacked, and the dealer deals tops and bottoms."

The salesman nodded, got in the cab and told the driver to take him to the pool hall where the "action" was.

"Hey, buddy," asked the driver, "didn't you hear what that redcap said? That's a crooked game."

"Well, take me there anyway. Hell, it's the only game in town, ain't it?"

I only quote this old gag to prove the point I was trying to make in my preceding chapter. If a man's a natural born gambler, he's going to gamble. Why shouldn't the millions upon millions of tax-free dollars that are lining the pockets of crooks every year in areas where gambling is not legal, go rather into the state coffers, and help our school systems, most of which are sadly in need of overhaul? Or state highways. Or be used, for that matter, in reducing personal taxes? Why not legalize gambling all over the country and eliminate income tax altogether? (Although I'm afraid the latter thought is mostly just wishful thinking.)

The most conservative area of the country, where the word "Yep" is considered a fair conversation, New England, was the first state to break the sound barrier. And if it can happen in New Hampshire, under the leadership of the ultra- conservative Governor John W. King, why shouldn't it happen in your state?

In a recent interview, Governor King expressed as his opinion that "it was a definite, basic human instinct for people to want to gamble."

He also, under further questioning, Governor King

said he thought laws opposing gambling are far too strict. He mentioned in particular the interruption by police of an informal, "at-home" poker game. So far as organized gambling goes, however, *unless* state operated, King is definitely opposed.

King, asked why of all the states, New Hampshire should be the first to conduct a state lottery, told reporters that "we've got more guts than many of your other states. And besides being known as ultra-conservative, in our outlook on most things we're very broadminded. We're liberal, for instance, in civil liberties. We've got a good clean record here, and while we don't boast about our virtues, we've got them."

Governor King admitted that he was surprised by the great amount of mail that arrived following passage of the new State lottery in New Hampshire. Mail from all over the country pours into his office daily. They've ceased to measure it by amount, now measure it by poundage. King says it's running "about 99.5 per cent in favor of a lottery for the writer's own state."

King also says that his legislature and legislators are, "he feels" a bit closer to the average man than in other states, where they'd be more likely to put in a sales tax to raise necessary funds. He says he'd veto any attempt to impose a sales tax on the people of New Hampshire.

King also favors making this movement, if it goes, a state's rights option, rather than to convert it to a national lottery. King feels that the money taken out of the state at present by the Federal government isn't being returned to the proper channels. He mentions as a specific the need for more federal school aid which, he claims is simply not forthcoming.

He admits to a great deal of local pressure *against* the new law, mostly from church groups and local civic organizations. He doesn't identify himself with these groups, but rather, in his own words, as more representative of the working classes, who favor it almost to the man.

King also feels that the lotteries will attract a lot of out-of-state money. Non-residents, as well as residents can buy these sweeps tickets. As it's against the law to send lottery tickets (for the purpose of sale) through the mail or to take them across state lines, or even to buy them knowing they have been so handled, a person would have to come to New Hampshire to buy their tickets, and he's presently awaiting a Federal ruling as to whether the person might then legally take his purchased ticket back across the state line to his home or if he will have to leave it there and return to New Hampshire to collect his money.

As it now stands, (and I'm not quoting Governor King) a ten per cent excise tax will have to be paid to the Federal government on every lottery ticket sold, and there's a strong rumor that Attorney General Robert Kennedy is dead set against the state lottery. King says he's felt no federal pressure as yet and doesn't really expect any.

There's no New Hampshire income tax, so a winner would only get bitten by a percentage of his winning by the U.S. tax boys.

King's plan calls for selling the tickets in the state's 69 state-operated liquor stores, but he thinks this is a solution rather than a problem, as the state-operated stores have an excellent record.

King also says that the horse racing people in his state are all for the bill. He says they form the strongest bloc in the assembly, and that if they'd opposed it, it wouldn't have had a chance of passing.

However, Governor King is dead set against any other form of legalized gambling, at least in the foreseeable future. "It tends to kind of get out of hand," he says, tersely.

King doesn't smoke, claims to be a lousy poker player, admits to an occasional drink, and as to his political future resulting from his approval of the controversial bill says blithely that "No one ever got rich in New Hampshire holding political office. I'm a practicing attorney, so I don't really care what happens."

In conjunction with this, it appears that Idaho is on the narrow edge of being made into a "completely" legalized state.

Also, it will be interesting to learn the ultimate results (which may well be known as you read this) of a poll conducted by a popular magazine with tremendous circulation that asks you to whether or not you, personally are for or against:

1. A National Lottery
2. Off-Track Betting
3. Monte-Carlo Type Casinos

Says this magazine, editorially: "It's time that our citizens stand up and be counted on the subject of wagering.

You may be sure there will either no or at best unfavorable response from the State of Nevada.

Why cut the rest of the country into a good thing?

Chapter XVI

"LAS VEGAS — THE CITY"

When you think of Las Vegas, you almost immediately think of the clink of silver dollars, the clatter of chips, the cries of *"Jackpot"* and of luxury shows at the most lavish casinos in the world. Well, all right, that's like we want you to think of it, but Vegas, if you know your way around, is a surprisingly inexpensive place to live.

Here's a sort of "Cook's Tour" of the *other* side of Las Vegas, the inexpensive side.

You see, the history of Las Vegas has a great deal

to do with the more "stable" elements of our citizenry. Until after the war, Vegas was little more than a railroad junction unvisited except by those making their way across the desert to and from the West Coast. Today, it's host to more than 10,000,000 tourists annually, and to tell you the truth, if you don't like to gamble, there's not much percentage in coming here at all, for there's no scenery and little other tourist activity.

Can you live in Las Vegas cheaply?

Yes. Almost everything in Vegas stays open twenty-four hours a day and by far the best bargains, including the cheaper foods, are to be found after midnight.

Three of the really best cheap hotels in Vegas are but a block or so from the Greyhound Terminal, and they're the Hotel Union, Hotel Monterey and Hotel Victory. The Union, 227 South Main, has 38 rooms and charges from $3.50 to $6 single occupany, a little higher for double occupancy. The Monterey, 303 South Main, which I consider to be a little nicer, starts at $3 single and scales upward. The Victory has rooms starting at $3.50 single and is located at 307 S. Main. It also offers connecting adjoining motel rooms for as little as $22.50 per week. There's another good hotel directly across from the bus terminal, the Sal Sagev, at 105 S. Main which is slightly better class and slightly higher-priced, starting at $6 single.

One of the nicer places to stop is, alas, one of the smallest, the Carson Hotel, at 316 Carson. It has only 8 small rooms, but if you should be lucky enough to get one it can cost you as little as $2.50 per day.

For a family, at better deal would be the MacDonald Hotel, 208 Las Vegas Blvd., North. Rooms for three for ten bucks and rooms for four at only $12. Rates go up about $1 on weekends.

As for motels, the best place to find the cheaper ones is on Las Vegas Blvd. (Highway 91) at the eastern part of town. I might mention the Emerald, 2091 Las Vegas Blvd., but there are a great many available in the lower brackets. Shop around, if you like.

As for food, that's plentiful and cheap in Las Vegas if you know where to look. The Fremont Hotel 200 Fremont in downtown Vegas, offers lunches from $1.25 to $1.50 and several BIG dinners at $2 or under. Better still, between 11:00 p.m. and 6 a.m., the Fremont offers what it calls its "Graveyard Special," offering ham and eggs at 65¢, spaghetti at 75¢ and several other entrees priced under $1.45 — the Strip is also a good place to eat cheaply in Vegas if you can only hang onto your appetite until midnight or later. That's when the top hotels, the luxury spots offer a buffet, which may vary from place to place in spots but usually is served western or "chuckwagon" style, allowing you all you can eat for $1.50 or less. A restaurant called Aku-Aku, near the Stardust hotel, has a Polynesian buffet at midnight for $1.50. Two other places on the strip, the New Frontier and the Silver Slipper offer 98¢ dinners! there's an extra charge for dessert and coffee at the New Frontier, though.

The Nevada Club, 109 Fremont with its 75¢ breakfasts is one of the liveliest places in town.

The whole idea being this: if you're on a short bankroll, you can actually sleep safely, cooly and comfortably and have a couple of good meals on as little as five bucks a day.

For cigarettes and "walking-around" money, though, you're on your own.

Here's a hint: one of the busiest places in town is the Western Union office is at 113 South Second Street, near the Golden Nugget. The telephone number is DU 2-4321, and it's always mighty crowded in there, partner, *mighty* crowded!

As for our townsfolk, they stay at home, rent apartments, or live in trailers. They grumble about their rents, the cost of steak,

One thing we don't grouse about is the taxes. There aren't any. And we think that's mighty nice.

So you see, we're just people. One dealer goes home to a nagging wife who wonders why he can't "catch on" as pit boss. Another weary bartender takes half his tips to the next casino and tries to improve his lot. A roulette dealer hurried to the supermarket to get in on the advertised specials, while still another stickman worries about his sick son.

Just plain people, with a job that's a little different from yours.

FLASH! As I was writing this page, news came to me that an attempt is being made to start the "sport of kings", horseracing, again in Las Vegas, after the last abortive attempt. On October 4, 1963, the gee-gees go again on the newest and "biggest little track" in the country. I write this as a book takes time to write, and so you won't think I'm a complete dunderhead. The track is called "Thunderbird Downs", just a whoop and a holler from Joe Wells' Thunderbird Hotel.

It's announced that there'll be (subject to state approval, of course) pari-mutuel wagering, a daily racing form and a regular betting "line".

The meet has been originally scheduled for five week ends of thoroughbred as well as quarterhorse racing throughout October and into the first couple of weeks of November.

It's a daring venture, to say the least, in view of the disastrous results of Las Vegas' first ill-fated attempt to lure the bettors away from the tables. And also, the debut will be bucking a red hot World Series. However, by the time this book is in print, we'll know what happened, won't we?

I personally predict another floperoo, but they might have something in those quarterhorse races at that. Sneeze, and you miss one of those races and you don't know whether you've won or lost until the odds are posted. That's almost as fast as the action at the craps tables, and if they fill in the lulls between starts with some of the well-developed chorus lines from the various shows around the strip, who knows?

Anyway, Joe E. Lewis will be a strong supporter, and his famous cry of "post time" will mean something else besides having another drink, now!

Chapter XVII

"ON THE SUBJECT OF PLAYING CARDS"

Now we come to the part of the book in which I really have an interest. Card playing. The good old pasteboards. In the casino's in France and Monte Carlo (Hi, there, Princess Grace!) they call them *l'ecartes,* or something that sounds very much like it, anyway, but it all falls into the same category.

Most of us have been subjected to the various games of cards at one time or another, as kids. "500 Rummy", "Old Maid", "Hearts", "Casino", "Seven Up" (the game, not the sparkling beverage), "Pinochle", "Solitaire, and Double Solitaire", "Cribbage" and Lord only knows what else.

Funny thing. You can teach a guy by example by showing him, exactly how to play dice or craps properly. The average guy, that is. If he started to play dice or shoot craps as a caddy, for example, and learned the hard way how to "PK" or "spin" the dice, he probably still fancies himself as pretty much of what we term a "mechanic". He's a line shooter, fades the other guy just enough to stay in the game, then picks up the dice, drops them until he finds his favorite way to pick them up, that is with sevens up and down and elevens around the edges. I can't explain this to you any further, but the guy who does it will recognize it from my description. Now, he's ready to go to work. On a blanket, at home, he can maybe even "run" the dice, and I've read and heard of and actually seen it done on a flat layout. That's to say, he can start by throwing twelve, then eleven, then ten, then nine, then eight, then seven, six, and so on down to a pair of aces, or "snake eyes". He can do this as many as nine times out of ten.

This guy, though, is dogmeat in a casino. We don't care *how* he throws the dice, backhand, underhand, spinning,trotting, pacing or pulling a milk wagon. Just as long as he hits the opposite rail, his chances of making a point are no better nor worse than yours. Watch the honest-to-God gambler in action, he hardly looks at the dice. He waits patiently for everyone to get their bets down, picks 'em up and tosses 'em.

Of course, we're not devoting this chapter to dice, I'm just telling you about the one guy who is incurable at a craps table. The most difficult thing in the world is to teach a man to play cards properly. You see, he's formed habit patterns in his mental processes as a child, and these aren't easy to shake loose. He might have a bankroll, a position of respect as an accountant in his own community, but at a card table he's still playing "Old Maid" or some such, and no matter what his *mind* tells him to do, what is a right bet and what is a wrong bet, his subconscious takes over.

At least, that's the way it seems to me. I have a few good friends and a number of more or less casual acquaintances who drop into Vegas once or twice a year, sometimes a little oftener, and they invariably ask my advice, but only after they've lost their shirts.

"I can't understand it," they'll say. "I just knew that dealer was bluffing at that 21 game, but he nailed me. Hell, I play blackjack (or gin, or poker) every Thursday at the country club back home, and I pride myself on being able to damn near tell how good a man's holding by the look on his face."

I try to explain to them that they're not playing some guy for his own bankroll. You can't bluff a dealer. There are certain ways he *must* play, to keep the house PC going, and he has unlimited funds. No matter how well you do or how poorly you do, he's only a working man, and at the end of his shift he collects his salary and goes home. I tell them "You're playing with your own money. *He's* playing with *units,* an a five-dollar chip doesn't mean a goddamned thing to him. He didn't buy it, if he wins it, fine, if he loses one to you he'll probably get it right back from someone else, and even if he doesn't, he doesn't care!"

This, of course, is one if the big reasons why the

casino customarily tops its allocated PC, which meets the nut and shows them a profit. Because that man behind the table has no more emotion about your money than a slot machine. If as much. He's NOT trying to beat YOU, as an individual. And so long as he stays within the rules laid down by the house, he cannot, in the long run, lose. Maybe to one player out of the six at his table, but on the overall scene, unless he's had a lousy shift indeed, he'll wind up winners, *just by playing the game the way he's told to play it.* He's the guy who absolutely must play by the house rules if he wants to keep his job. You, of course, are free to do anything you like.

And generally, when you do, it's against all the laws of playing winning cards.

That's lesson one.

Lesson number two would start something like this: try, although it's difficult, to develop your memory. The more cards you can remember *being played,* the more accurate you're going to be in making your next selection, whether it be a hit, a draw or, as in gin, a pick. Don't *depend* on your memory, because it will often fail you in a card game unless you've literally had years of practice at it. But try, that's the main thing. It will help your game.

Next, as in all other gambling, know your odds for and against a winning combination. In other words, KNOW the game before you play it. You'd be surprised how many grown men I've seen get into a poker game not knowing whether or not a full house will beat a flush, or if a flush will beat four of a kind. Happens every day. The excuse is: "Gee, I haven't played for so long that . . .", and that's no excuse at all, is it? Really?

Another question I'm frequently asked is: Whom do I consider to be the greatest card player in the world today? I can answer that one easily unless, God forbid, he should drop dead before I finish this book. He's a guy who looks more like an accountant than a gambler, a man who moves in the best social circles, a man who is just as much at home in a high-stake poker game as in a polite bridge tournament. He has one vice, and believe it or not it isn't money. I've seen him get up and say, "Sorry, kid. You don't know enough about the game to play me" and mean it, even if the "pigeon" is begging to be plucked.

His sole vice is in wanting to beat the toughest players he can come up against, and he'll travel a thousand miles to trim some guy who has a big local reputation. For money, marbles or chalk, I may add. He has a mind like an IBM, and I'll never forget the first time I saw him go up against a so-called "tough" gambler in Kansas City. The stakes were high. The game was gin.

This man I'm touting as the greatest sat through a couple of games, winning about two grand. The deal opened for the third game, and the big tough gambler from the midwest discarded and picked one. My boy picked one and discarded. On the third pick, my man looked at the tough player and said: "I'd like to make you a little side bet. For a grand. It's getting late and I've got to catch a plane back to the Coast in the morning. You shouldn't even be playing this game, because you don't know a damned thing about it."

Mr. Big huffed and puffed and asked what the bet was for and about.

"I'll tell you exactly what cards you're holding. *Now.*"

The slightly puzzled midwesterner looked at his hand, grinned, said "That's a bet."

"Fine," my man said. "Now. I'll put my finger on them, the rest of the table can get in back of you and watch. I'll point to the card from the back and tell you what it is. If I make one mistake, you don't owe me a dime on the night and I'll buy the drinks. That's a better bet than you took. In other words, I'm giving you two to one."

That rubbed a salt in the wound.

"Start!"

My man calmly, without the least hesitation, called all the cards the man was holding by suit and color and size. (That's a little redundant, but you must realize I was a little excited and awed at this point, and I guess it still hangs on.)

"That's three grand you owe me," said my boy, unruffled. "I'll do it one more time, you deal, double or nothing. Or else give me my three grand and I'll be on my way."

The big, tough player from the midwest huffed and puffed and backed down.

"I've got fifteen minutes before I have to start on the way to the airport." His eyes looked challengingly around the room, "I'll give anybody in the room the same bet for a dollar. One dollar, even up."

There was a dead silence until the colored boy who'd been held over to mix and serve the refreshments (my man doesn't drink, by the way) coughed with some embarrassment. "If none of y'all gentlemen don't want it, I'd like to try a little of that action."

Everyone said, laughing, "Get in there, Willy, and clean him out!"

Willy wound up winning five hundred bucks. In just a few minutes by doubling up, letting his winning ride, etc.

Now, lo and behold! The midwestern sharpshooter got up a little courage, finally figuring that just the sheer size of the bets had been what had kept him down, challenged my boy to make any kind of card bet, even money, he cared to make.

"Make three picks and I'll tell you what you're holding and where you're holding them in your hand."

He also added the words "Cash, of course. I don't play for checks or markers."

My man put up three thousand in cash on the table, told a pop-eyed Willy to get three more from Mr. Tough, and just slide the money over to the winner. "Okay with you if Willy holds out five hundred for himself?", my boy asked.

"Okay, *okay!*"

"Who'll deal?"

"Anyone in the room but you or me."

My man nodded. "How about you?" The man so indicated shuffled and dealt.

The "tough" midwesterner made his three picks, so did my boy.

My man went through the same routine. I might add this was a fresh deck. He picked up $5,500 and said goodnight, all around, his hand still face down on the table. "Oh," he added, as an afterthought, "care to make some kind of bet on *my* hand? Double or nothing that you can't name even two cards correctly in my hand and never mind where they are?"

The midwesterner, deflated moneywise as well as suffering from a ripped, torn and battered ego, turned his back and went to the men's room, without bothering to answer.

"I guess we may as well leave then," my man said. "Jack, are you going to the coast? I understand that this is a light flight tonight."

I shook my head, figuring that if this cat's luck ever changed, I was a dead pigeon on that plane.

He got back, all right, and he's still on the prowl today. Watch out for him. He's equally good at poker, bridge or gin, although I think he's the greatest gin player I've ever seen in action, and I just hope he doesn't give my real name away, because I can tell you he knows it, and that all this action was made up (but not played) at Blue Hills Country Club in Kansas City, Missouri.

My sincere advice to you: no matter how tough you think you may be at playing cards (and name your game) look out for a fellow who closely resembles an accountant and looks about as deadly as a chocolate milk shake.

His name is Oswald Jacobi.

The greatest memory player of them all.

He knows the law of odds (indeed, he may well have written it), the laws of probabilities, and everytime a card is flashed, even the *corner* of a card, his IBM brain registers whether it's red or black, a number or a face card.

He isn't tough.

He's the greatest card player I've ever seen in my life, and I know all the names of the so-called "greats".

He doesn't cheat, use "readers," "slicks" or "strippers".

He doesn't need this sort of aid. God gave him a brain that was meant for just one thing — figures. Some insurance company should have him on their payroll, I believe, just as golf equipment outfits sponsor pro golfers.

Why, I can even hear the commercials now:

If Oswald Jacobi says it's a good bet to take our Automobile Insurance, you can DEPEND *on it!"*

And then I can visualize Jacobi looking up, at the screen, smiling blandly and saying, "That's right folks. And we'll pay you double or nothing!"

Oswald Jacobi. Greatest of them all.

His income had been estimated at various figures, although I'm sure he files an honest tax return, as from $35,000 to $100,000 per year, in addition to expenses.

He could, I'm sure, make a lot more if he sought out pigeons. But he won't. The money is secondary. He loves to find a guy who can give him some real competition.

What to know something?

Every year we hold the International Jacobi Gin Rummy Tournament in Las Vegas. It was Oswald's dream child.

Guess who's barred from participating?

That's right!

Jacobi!

Chapter XVIII

"HOW TO PLAY WINNING GIN"

As I explained before, this is a pretty ticklish subject, telling anyone who is suffering from a childhood fixation or "trauma" on how to change their style of play, or even discard it altogether in order to start a new one. Yet, sometimes *winning* gin goes against all your instincts.

Like, if you're drowning at sea, and instead of the lifeguard throwing you a preserver he shouts "Dive, you fool!" it somehow doesn't ring a bell. You feel that somewhere along the line you've been had, right?

This often happens in gin.

The object of the game is simple. To beat your opponent.

The object of a fighter pilot during the war was the same, and yet the same figuring still applies. Your "common sense" may tell you to do something that's altogether wrong.

Personally, as the lesser of two evils (flying fighters

and playing gin) would, to me, be sticking to the card game. Yet, unless you know not only the rules, the laws of averages but have, as well, the instinct for the game, you'll get "shot down" as surely as the fighter pilot who pulls up when he should have dived, although every nerve-end and muscle in his body was screaming "pull up".

So it goes with gin.

Gim rummy is a very tough game. It's a modern game, evolved from all the laborious games of rummy that have sprung up since granpop was a young'n, and is just about the ultra-ultra in refinement.

"I just can't throw (discard) a safe card", one guy sighs. "I might as well give up the game."

Well now, let's call a screeching halt right here and examine things. What's this guy talking about? More importantly, *WHEN* is he talking about? Early or late in the game?

Early in the game is, unquestionably, the toughest time to discard. Unless you're a very lucky guy, indeed, this will often tip your opponent as to what you're looking for, hoping to make, or trying to fish for.

But remember this: neither you nor your opponent will try to break up a possible or actual combination on his very first discard. Suppose you hold the Jack-ten of diamonds, and a pair of unrelated Queens, in your hand. You're unlikely to throw any of those four cards as a discard on your very first toss, right?

Naturally, the most stupid discard you can make is one of the Queens or either your unrelated Jack or ten.

This is also true of your opponent, and this is where the Jacobi (or IBM) system comes into effect. The common way to open a gin game is as follows:

Each player gets ten cards. Now, in the normal, or ordinary gin game, the top card (after the deal) is turned up. Let's say it's a six. The player who is not dealing has a choice of picking it up. If he declines, then the dealer can take a shot at it. If *HE* declines, then the other player picks from the top of the deck.

Right away you know sixes aren't of much account to either of you.

Now you have some information as to the dealer's hand. Use that information *to make the safest possible discard.*

Obviously, any six is a reasonably safe discard, unless the dealer in this instance is " fishing for a six". Still, you have the edge when you discard. Obviously, he isn't fishing for THAT six, or he'd have taken it. So maybe he's fishing for another six. The odds, are, however, that he isn't fishing at all. What's more, you may not have another six at that time, so that he can be filling, or even planning to fill another six for a sequence.

And, let's take one thing at a time. No early discard *is entirely* safe. But one thing you know by now. You don't want a six and neither does he. Nevertheless, if it's safe against three of a kind, as you know it must be, unless you're playing a complete and utter idiot, it's not necessarily safe against a sequence.

Later on, just to prove you know the game, when you have to discard, your best discard is a King. Next best is a Queen. If you don't hold or can't spare a

King or Queen, you're on your own, and here's why: The King can fit only into a *downward* sequence. KING-Queen-Jack. The Queen can fit into either a downward or upward sequence QUEEN, Jack, Ten, or King-QUEEN-Jack. Any other high card may fit a downward, upward or middle sequence. A Jack may fit any of these sequences. JACK-Ten-Nine, Ten-JACK-Queen, or King-Queen-JACK.

In other words, most cards fit into three sequences. A King into only one, a Queen into two. The same thing goes for Aces and deuces.

Also, remember this, to put the odds in your favor. Say the seven of spades, for example, is the discard. Then the six or eight of spades is a reasonably safe next discard. This stops the sequences from going in three different ways instead of just one.

However, and this is most important if you're to play the game at all, get RID of a useless King or Queen at the first possible moment, or you might just find yourself giving your opponent more time to accumulate picture cards, which makes it much less safer to discard. In fact, you might even be stuck with it for the entire hand, which is doing you nothing but harm.

Is there a rule to follow when it's *your* turn to deal?

Don't make me laugh. There's a rule when you're dealing that's worth a million bucks. (What a bargain this book is, hey?).

Let's say the up card is something like a five, and neither player wants it. Your opponent draws first from the deck and discards, we'll say, a ten of clubs. You're holding the Jack of clubs and the eight of hearts as your (until then) "useless" cards. Which would you discard after his play?

Would the eight of hearts be safer? Of course not.

Forget that tempting little old ten laying on the discard pile. Remember: if your opponent had another ten, or anything "to" the ten, he wouldn't have tossed away part of a combination on the very first discard. Discard your Jack.

Now, how can your opponent use it? In the first place, he can make three Jacks, but that's unlikely, as he wouldn't have broken up a Jack-ten sequence on the very first discard. Second, he might be able to use it in an *upward* sequence, Jack - Queen - King, but this is a toughy and the odds are against it. We know he can't use it downwards, as *he* threw away the ten himself.

Figuring out the odds, without going into detail, I'll tell you here and now that your discard following his, in the manner above discribed, gives you an immediate two-to-one edge over him.

General rule for discarding: After your opponent discards, (his first discard, that is) your best bet is always to discard in a different suit and as close to the rank of his discard as possible.

If I were to set forth a few rules regarding winning at gin rummy, they would fall in this sequence:

1. What I just told you about first discards.

2. Memorize, for *sure,* as many cards as you can that have been in play.

3. Stay away from a "pattern". Don't play low cards all the time simply because your opponent dumps them all the time. Nor don't play high cards all the

time for the same reason. In other words, don't establish a "pattern" in your play that can be used against you.

4. Again, remember. Gin is a game of memory as well as luck and skill on the discard. Twenty-one of the fifty-two cards in the deck are immediately known between the two of you as soon as you deal.

You know what eleven of them are, he knows what eleven of them are. After one of you makes the first discard, the odds go up in your opponent's favor, as he now knows not only the actual faces of 12 of the cards in the fifty-two card deck, he also has an inkling of what you may have in your hand, or what you're looking for. The player who makes the first discard, therefore, is always at a slight disadvantage.

5. A good rule to go by: if you can "knock" on ten or less after only two or three picks, do it. The odds are in your favor, but decline sharply after picks number four and five. (By this time, 41 cards of the 52 will have been in play, and you better start looking for some small cards, unless you're certain, dead certain that your opponent holds higher cards than you and can't get help from either you or the deck).

6. Forget "schneiders". If you get one fine, it's like falling over a five dollar bill on the sidewalk. If you start deliberately to go for them, you're inviting disaster.

7. A cardinal rule. Never practice this game against your wife. She'll beat you every time and give you the damndest inferiority complex you've ever had.

8. Don't talk too much when you're playing. Let the other guy keep the conversation rolling. Even

when he begs: "Let this next one be big and bold", you can tell, after he's made that or similar remarks a few times that he's really trying to con you out of tossing a low card.

9. And most important. *Don't* play gin with anyone if it's going to hurt you financially to lose, depending on the predetermined stakes. I've seen many a good player go to the wall because he simply couldn't afford to lose that next hand.

Don't, for a minute think that gin's an easy game to play or an easy game to teach. It's neither.

I would say, however, you don't have to be an Oswald Jacobi to get a big kick out of the game, which is, after all a kind of glorified "Knock rum", which you probably played as a kid, just for laughs.

When you're playing for money, and a half-cent a point, even, could amaze you, it's a different game altogether, and you'd do well to watch thoroughly before you get your own feet wet.

Otherwise,you might find yourself head-deep instead of just ankle deep in a thing that looked so easy.

I like to play an occasional game of gin, but I don't recommend it as a way of life, except to guys like Jacobi. (In my heart, I *hate* the bum!).

Chapter XIX

"MORE ABOUT CARDS"

I've saved all this hoo-hah about cards and card games until the latter portion of this book for one very simple reason: this is my favorite gamble, and I flatter myself I know at least a little about cards and card games.

Here are a few rules of the road I've learned as I've gone through life. I pass this advice along to you, although you may or may not take it. Remember this is the voice of experience speaking.

First, don't play pinochle with an older man. Unless you've played this game and this game ONLY for the greater part of your life, he'll murder you. It's sort of like snooker pool. You don't see much of it around anymore, and it's the old timers who'll kill you at it.

Second, don't play with strangers, *ever,* under any circumstances, unless you, yourself, are a hustler. First thing, they wouldn't want you in the game if they didn't mean to hustle you, and that's the truth.

Also, don't play with your friends, unless you know them very well indeed. It's an easy way to lose them. I know!

Next thing, listen and watch (especially in poker games) for odd sounds, ear pullings, twitching of the eyes, nervous coughs, "aimless" whistling. This often means two or more confederates are letting each other know what they're holding.

Also, watch the shuffle and deal. If the dealer is using a "mechanic's" grip, which means the deck is pretty well concealed in his hand with the thumb hooked over the leading edge, he's probably dealing crooked. Don't make a scene. Just suddenly remember a prior appointment, get up and leave. Tell everyone a pleasant "good night" and take it on the heel and toe.

Another good time to stop and take stock of the mess you may find yourself in is when a player consistently (I'd call this one more time than once) drops cards during the play. In this case, again, while it may just be a nervous gesture, a twitch, so to speak on his part, you're playing with your own money. Leave nicely and politely, but *leave.*

Never play cards with women. You can't bluff them, because they can't understand the rules of the game. They lack a native caution, to begin with, and delight in games like "One-eye" Jacks, "Spit in the Ocean", and such. This is not gambling. This is ridiculous.

Never worry about any of these things when you go up against the house in Vegas, or anywhere in Nevada. You'll get an honest deal, even if you don't win.

A great many dealers in Nevada can manipulate the cards pretty well, dealing seconds or tops and bottoms. Dealing tops and bottoms is so simple a move that I could teach it to you in five minutes. I can spot it at a distance of ten feet in ten seconds, and I'm no more a card dealer than I am a bullfighter. This is strictly forbidden, and carries a heavy penalty if a dealer is ever caught cheating. So heavy, in fact, that it literally doesn't happen.

You might notice, in a casino game, how closely the dealer will watch the hands of an obvious "smoothy", someone he's got spotted for a sure fire cheater. This guy will have super-sharpened finger nails. He'll either make a slight scratch on all aces and big cards as he can in say, three or four rounds of the cards, or he'll use some other identification mark. The dealer may spot this right off the bat, and when the guy tosses a five dollar chip out there instead of the silver dollar he's *been* betting, the dealer will pull the cards and start with a fresh deck. When the pit boss comes by, the dealer hands him the deck, nods quietly at the man in question, and if he's been up to some monkey business, he'll be barred from the club for life. Some cheaters use what's called "daub" under their fingernails, and while a sharp dealer can usually catch on to this in a hurry, it's pretty hard to detect white on white. Nevertheless, the *sequence* of the cheater's betting will make him suspicious, and once again the dealer will open a new deck.

I've seen really good dealers change cards time after time, while the cheater grimly hangs on, sort of hoping that he's not really being understood. Meanwhile, the dealer will have taken him for a nice little bundle while this cheater is waiting to get into action.

There's a lot more information I could dish out about cheating, but I don't want to start you on a career of crime.

I will say this, and it's perfectly acceptable and understood by all hands concerned: If you catch a dealer "asleep at the switch", so to speak, take full advantage of it. This isn't cheating, isn't regarded as cheating or even as dirty pool. In fact, he'd laugh at the poor boob who failed to take advantage of a bad error he, the dealer, had made by not maintaining his vigilance at all times which is an important part of his job.

Now, let's see where we are. What's your favorite Gin? game? Poker? Blackjack? Chemin de Fer? Bridge?

Chances are, your favorite game is the one you need help with, because you *will have established certain mental "patterns"* which will make your play, your reaction, as it were, almost automatic and often wrong.

Don't forget this: every hand is a new game. You're starting over. While the odds actually change in Chemin de Fer, as the cards are dealt, or in 21 or Blackjack, they're of little or no significance to anyone except an expert "memory" player such as Jacobi, Mike Goodman, Ed Thorpe and several others. Even the dealer pays little or no attention to this aspect of changing odds, unless or until he discovers, with a start, that he's bucking a memory player.

Now, most people think that a dealer in 21 must play all the way through the deck before reshuffling, but this simply isn't true. He can shuffle any time he wants to. And, more importantly, you can call for a reshuffle any time you think *you've* spotted a memory player (no particular reason why it should bother you, though) or at any time you feel like it. You can also request that a new deck be put in play, and often as not the dealer will do it for you, although he isn't compelled to do so.

Same thing holds true in a crap game. If you think the dice are too "cold", not passing often enough to suit you, when your turn to shoot comes up you can toss the dice to the dealer and ask for a new pair. He'll extend a box to you to make your own pick. Incidentally, two minor items that might be of interest to you. When cards are withdrawn from a game, unless damaged, they're not thrown away by the house. They're carefully washed and cleaned, and put back into play. Scratched or nicked cards, naturally, are destroyed. And if you want a pair of house dice to take home, you can't buy them. Just ask the pit boss and he'll give you a pair. No charge, no tip.

Back to cards, including etiquette. In poker, it isn't considered quite *kosher* to "check" then bet or raise the hand. Don't worry about it. You'll do it once with a real gambler, and you'll never do it again.

If the cards come to you for a cut, *cut*. Maybe you don't want to, but maybe all the other players in the game want those cards cut. And when you're getting down to the rub, where everyone has dropped out but you and your opponent, *don't show your hand to another player at the table* until all betting is done and the winner decided. It's against the rules of poker, and while no one may say anything to you about it, it's illegal according to Hoyle, and if your opponent calls you for doing it, you lose the pot.

Also, in poker as well as any other gambling game, make sure you know what the chips are worth before you set in. Many a player, because of false pride, has stayed with a game about three deals and slunk away with his tail between his legs because his bankroll was too short for the game he busted into. Don't be afraid to ask the going rates. If you're on short money, no one's to sneer at you. They've all been there, too, remember.

Above all, don't listen to "kibitzers". These are the guys who go "tsk, tsk" when you make a draw or a discard that they don't approve of. Or who groan "Oh, no!" when you drop out, and advise you that you'd have won if you'd only taken one card, or if you'd held the kicker.

Personally, I've never seen a kibitzer worth a damn on the infrequent occasions he gets a little bankroll. He'll get in a game, and all his profound knowledge that makes him the "expert" when he's breathing down your neck suddenly disappears. I suspect, not without reason, that the "expert" knowledge wasn't there in the first place. These guys are like touts at the race track. They get their kicks by watching *you* sweat, but when they've got their own money on the line they're the last guys in the world to seek advice even if they probably need it more than anyone else.

It's considered perfectly allowable for you to turn around in your chair in a card game and tell a kibitzer, politely, to "Please get the hell out of my hair. Go bug someone else!"

I consider this next piece of advice childish to give, but I suppose it's something that's happened to all of us at one time or another. Good old George, a great guy and a dead game player, goes bust. Rather than relinquish his seat, he looks over at you, if you're piling up the chips in front of you, and says: "Sam, let me take a hundred. I'll give you back a hundred and a quarter."

Well, some of that money in front of you used to belong to good old George. Besides, you know he's good for the loan. It's a hard thing to do, especially if you're not going to miss the amount he aks you for, but remember this: you raise the odds against yourself some twenty-percent in a five or six handed game, because *you'll be playing against your own money*. Remember, also, the first axiom of gambling. Once you buy chips, they don't belong to anyone until there's a final decision reached in the game. So, in effect, you're not only lending George a hundred out of YOUR pile — you're also lending him chips that are as much the property of the other players as they are yours. They just happen to be in front of you at that particular time.

You've just got to learn to say "no," politely but firmly. Let good old George go elsewhere for his fresh bankroll, and welcome him back into the game warmly, but don't let him borrow money from you. If someone else at the table wants to do it, fine and dandy. Let them. Best thing for you to do, then, is to cash in, win or lose, and take it on the well-known heel and toe. Go elsewhere for your action, because you can't get a decent rattle for your money going up against guys who lend it back and forth during a game.

More advice: don't play cards in your own home town, where gambling isn't legal, in an "after hours" spot. Man, they've got "readers" on sale at the local magician's supply shop that a trained eye can spot clear across the room. The craps layout, too, is more than likely crooked, what with "shapes", "trims", "right or wrong" dice, etc.

I don't care who touts you off on this game. Most of them have guys out hustling up trade who are known as "ropers," and they haunt the bars and hotel lobbies around town "steering" the tourist or well-heeled drunk into one of these games. Sometimes, if you're flashing enough lettuce around and seem to be drunk enough to not have full use of all your faculties, they'll back off everyone but housemen, and work you over so fast and so quickly that you'll wonder what happened when you sober up.

The "roper" gets from 10% to 25% of your losses, so they aren't planning on giving you a fair shake at anything. But some of the stories are awfully good, the stories these "ropers" use.

"It's a bartender and waiter's club", he'll say confidentially. "You can't get in unless you've got a union card, see?" And he'll show you his. "Just a place where the bartenders can go after hours when they get off shift. You gotta show a card or be with a cardholder to get in. And these guys don't make enough to make it a real tough game, know what I mean? A fellow holding four or five hundred bucks can clean up in there. Listen, I'll take you along with me, if you slip me ten per cent of your winnings, okay?"

It's a good story, isn't it? And there are a hundred more just as good. A story for every occasion. Alas and alack, they all have the same unhappy ending. "Guess it just wasn't your night, old buddy. Here, have a drink on me. Any place I can drop you off?"

You'd be surprised at how many suckers are so completely taken in by this gaff that they literally beg to come back for more of the same. Human nature is sure funnny. A guy who makes five or six hundred bucks a week naturally feels he's sharper than a bunch of $90 a week bartenders and waiters. What he doesn't understand is the fact that in many towns you can join the bartenders or waiters union for fifty or a hundred bucks, pay your dues every month and not even know how to open a bottle of beer. Of course, there are plenty of real bartenders and waiters in these joints, and the operators let them win a little and lose a little, so that they'll keep coming back. Additionally, there are the guys who like to drink after they get off shift, and of course these joints keep a few jugs of bourbon and Scotch around. Average retail cost, $5 per bottle. Average shot, one ounce, sells for a buck. Profit from a quart of booze (which holds 32 ounces) is a lousy $27, and that's not too hard to take, either.

There are a great many more of these joints than you'd imagine. Usually, they're in private homes, well-isolated. And you *can't* get in unless you hold a bartender's card. Also, if a vice cop should go to the trouble of buying a union card, which isn't too likely, and gets into the joint, it's just a private party so far as he can see, because a stranger is automatically suspect, even one brought in by a roper, who can usually smell "fuzz" at fifty yards, so that no money changes hands while there's a stranger in the house.

Hell, it's just a private party, and if you have one every night, it's just that the boys chipped in and bought a few jugs. And even if you should get busted, the first time it's only a misdemeanor, carrying a $250 fine. Of course, in some towns the cops are working hand-in-glove with this set-up, while in others they simply turn a blind eye on it, because of the difficulty of getting any sort of conviction. Why bother?

A friend (maybe I should say ex-friend) of mine once got himself trapped into one of these layouts. They wiped him out in an hour or two, and he gnashed his teeth for a week. Why? Because he was a professional gambler, wise to every trick of the trade. Trouble was, he'd been playing with honest cards, dice and odds for so long where gambling is as legal as operating a clothing store, that he'd temporarily forgotten about crooked cards and dice. When he realized what a trap he was in, he left quietly. which is the smartest thing to do. What he did wrong, and all he did wrong (for we can all make honest mistakes) was to go around telling his friends about it and they all laughed at him, for he was considered to be a very hep character and a tough guy to go up against at any time.

The reason these joints play as crooked as they do, as opposed to the strict honesty which prevails in Vegas, is volume.

We operate 24 hours a day, and have people waiting in line with their money in their sweaty little palms, just drooling to get at the action, whereas they have to go out and *hunt* customers. They seldom get into action before two o'clock in the morning, when the bars close, and shut down by six or seven, same morning, when the bars open again.

I've seen these joints try to run honest, to give you a real shot for your money, and hope to make up the difference on liquor sales. A couple of boys from Vegas got the idea, and found themselves an ideal set-up, a well-secluded house, the works. The word went out that this was an honest game, run Vegas style, with Vegas dealers. It was, too. They folded in a couple of weeks. No volume, and they couldn't bring themselves to operate a dishonest game.

"Even the cops came around," one of them told me, later, "and told us on the q.t. that they knew we were in action and having trouble getting off the ground and understood we were running a square game, even if it was against the law. They had plenty of other after-hour joints they could have busted, and offered to do it, if it would help us. They didn't want money. They simply knew there was always going to be gambling, and they'd much rather have their eyes on one decent joint than a dozen scurvy ones. We declined. Everyone's entitled to make a buck is the way I look at it, and to lose it any way he prefers."

The boys came limping back to Vegas, and are currently working. They're considered good men, who'll play you tough but honest, and that's the sort we want in Vegas.

But we were talking about cards. First, let's take a look at a game that's partly luck (as are all card games) and partly skill, plus a smidgin of the knowledge of human psychology. That's poker, and that's what the next chapter is all about.

Chapter XX

"POKER — THE ODDS AND THE GAME"

No matter what game you play — poker, 21, roulette, or name it — there are certain irrefutable and unchangeable laws of chance, or odds.

These may vary from play to play, hand to hand, night to night, but they always work out exactly — and I do mean exactly — the same way. You can't improve upon them, you can't change them. You can only go along with them, understand them, and know when they're working *for* you or *against* you.

This is a fact.

You can be the roughest, toughest player in the world, but you can't change the law of averages. Sometimes you can make this law work *for* you, other times it will work against you, with absolutely no help on your part. Push a light switch and the light goes on. Turn on the tap and the water runs. 99 and 9/10th's percent of the time. It's that small fraction that can throw you, cost you, knock you right out of the box. That last 1/10th.

This sort of figuring can make the difference between losing and winning poker.

Poker, card-wise, is a very simple game.

It's popularly supposed to be either a game of skill or a game of chance. There's a story that goes around which says that there was a trial about this very thing. If poker was a game of skill there was no gambling involved. If not, if it was a game of chance, about four or five guys were going to jail. They tied up the jury with a deck of cards for the night, and the decision came out eight to four that it was a game of chance. Curiously, the four (the jury was polled) who said it was a game of *Skill,* were the winners. The eight losers called it "gambling" and "game of chance" all the way.

It wound up a no-decision court battle, and didn't really settle anything except this: odds are odds. It may take a little longer for odds to show in poker than in other games, but the odds are there, all right, as immovable and undeniable as the Rock of Gibraltar.

This won't do you a bit of good unless you know how to take advantage of these odds. There's such a thing as a "hopeless" poker hand, naturally, but you shouldn't telegraph the fact to your opponents. You should even *drop* a couple of units (forget the word "money" while you're in the action) partly to show your ignorance, partly to show you don't chicken out too easily, even if you know, from *these* same irrefutable laws of average that you simply can't win.

Don't let the other guy get too confident, in other words. While you're bidding and betting, you set the pace of the game. Remember this. It's important.

I would say that a reasonably good poker player, in a 25 cent ante game, should pick up, knowing the odds and more importantly, *playing*-the odds should make somewhere between $75 to $100 per week, working a five day week, six to eight hours per day. Not a fortune, that's true, but a nice sum, with only a small investment.

* * *

Let's take a look at an "honest" poker game. A game in which there are no "daubs," "trims," or other gaffed arrangements, including crooked dealing.

Now, we're talking about honest hands, received by the player in an honest 52-card game.

What are the chances of catching certain types of hands when five honest cards are dealt out to each player? At a later date we can analyze the various games of poker in which one or more of the original cards may be discarded and replaced by the draw.

Now we come into some rather wild figures. A deck consists of 52 cards, Poker is essentially, and basically, a five card game. Get ready.

There are 2,598,960 different possible poker hands in the selection of five cards from the 52-card deck.

Of these random hands, 1,302,540 or more than half the entire number of hands (or possibilities) are dealt, on the overall average, with no pair or higher showing on the deal.

We call these "busts." Other hands will contain one

pair, two pair, and so on. Following is a table that indicates the chance of a poker player to receive the types of hands listed.

God help you, unless you've got a memory like our old friend Oswald Jacobi, this won't be of much help to you. Nevertheless, working from a total of a little more than a quarter of a million deals, which should be a fair indication of averages, your chances for drawing certain types of poker hands on the original deal, goes like this:

ODDS FOR POKER HANDS

Hand	*Odds Against Getting*
Royal Flush	649,789 to 1
Straight Flush	72,192 to 1
Four of a Kind	4,164 to 1
Full House	693 to 1
Flush	508 to 1
Straight	254 to 1
Three of a Kind	46 to 1
Two Pairs	20 to 1
One Pair	4 to 3
Busts	1 to 1

As I said, unless you have an IBM mind, these laws of probability are going to get away from you — altogether. To simplify it, let's put it this way — one hand higher than two pairs occurs once in every 35 times, meaning that the odds against getting such a hand are 34 to 1.

From time to time it might behoove you to check

the above table for the odds and probabilities for other specified hands.

*   *   *

DRAW POKER

There are so many ways to play poker, so many different variations that it simply isn't possible to put them into one book. However, the basic game of poker is, beyond all dispute, 5-card draw, so let's discuss it here and now.

Five cards are dealt to each player by the dealer. (If you didn't already know that, you shouldn't be reading these books for big boys). In proper rotation, any player holding a pair of Jacks or better is allowed (if it's his turn to open) to initiate a procedure whereby each other player is (after dropping a bet into the "ante," which is a predetermined figure) entitled to draw one, two or three cards, after discarding the same number of cards. AFTER discarding.

The player who does this is said to "open" the game, or hand. Or draw.

See if you can remember these odds in relation to playing. I'm sorry if you've paid out your good, hard-earned money for another book which quotes the same odds, but up is up and down is down, no matter how much or how little you pay for the information. So.

Each player in a five-card game (5-handed, too) of poker has exactly 1 chance in 5 — 1 chance in 5, no more, no less — of getting a pair of Jacks or better in the opening deal of the five original cards he's been dealt.

Take all the figures, without getting into decimal points and this means simply that one in five hands may be a pair of Jacks or better, which is exactly what we've said.

Next, as a player, you naturally want to know how to improve your hand. Suppose you discard three, hold two and draw three cards. Odds against bettering your hand at all, in any way shape or form are 7-3 against. The odds against your making certain combinations are like this (and again, these are not MY figures, nor are they anyone's figures; they're the laws of chance and probability, and no way has been found of breaking them).

Making two pairs	5 to 1
Making three of a kind	8 to 1
Making a full house	89 to 1
Making four of a kind	360 to 1

Remember, these odds are just as much against the player as you, which should give you some guidance in your betting, right?

If you hold one card and a "kicker," generally an Ace, and draw only two cards, then you have the following set of odds going against your bettering your hand:

Making two pairs	4½ to 1	(a bit better)
Making three of a kind	12 to 1	(much worse)
Making a full house	120 to 1	(worse)
Making four of a kind	1080 to 1	(forget it)

The odds against bettering the hand at all are approximately 3 to 1. You can see, by comparing the overall picture above, there's a disadvantage rather than an advantage in holding a "kicker." The chance of making two pairs increases only slightly, while the other possibilities *decrease* sharply.

I think it's safe to say it isn't too smart to hold a kicker in a game of 5-card draw poker.

Should you discard the lower of two pairs to improve your hand? Some people say "yes," others say "no." I'm afraid to say I belong to the latter group.

While the odds hover around 11 to one to improve two pairs with a one card discard and draw, consider this: the only possible improvement is a full house. Which is a 90-1 bet against on the original deal.

Also, the odds against bettering a three card draw are as follows:

Bettering the pair	2½ to 1
Making two pairs	5 to 1
Making a hand higher than two pairs	7 to 1

Remember, though, if these tables of odds tend to confuse you, that you make a sacrifice when you discard the lower of two pairs to make a three-card draw. If you're convinced that it's going to take something better than you're holding, say Jacks and fives, to win, your action might be justified, in view of your opponent's play and the cards you've seen exposed (because you'll always see *some*) you might be justified in lessening your chances, and raising your odds in order to make a sure-fire losing hand into a possible winner.

However, you're not playing poker in such a case, you're playing "finesse," or what I'd call "hope and Pray."

If you're convinced that two pair might win the hand,

discard your off card and go for broke. Remember, a hand consisting of two pairs happens on the average of only once every 27 times. Think of that. Remember that figure. One in every 27 times.

Now, let's suppose you draw three of a kind. Here are the odds against bettering this hand:

Against a full house	15 to 1
Against 4 of a kind	22½ to 1
Against even bettering the hand	11 to 1

In any combination of draw, the odds are not increased by holding a kicker, and as a factual look at the tables should convince you, the odds on getting four of a kind is considerably decreased, while the chance of getting a full house (depending on the kicker you hold, naturally) remains about the same. So, don't hold a kicker.

And remember, the odds are working for or against your opponents just as they're working for or against you.

LET'S DISCUSS FLUSHES — AND STRAIGHTS

You have one chance in 5 to draw a single card to 4 others in order to make a flush. Your chances are even less in drawing a single card to fill a straight, even an open-end straight. The chance of getting either end of a straight is approximately 6 to 1 against.

On inside straights, the odds are formidable. 12 to 1 against, although if you, like me, have ever tried one you'd bet the odds were even worse.

Smart gamblers, I hear, never draw — *never* — to an inside straight.

How do you bet against someone who draws a single card, considering that he's bucking the same odds as you? It's advisable to go against him for one bet, just to see if he's talking or playing, but it isn't advisable to go beyond that point. You see, you're playing, now, a combination of skill, luck, odds and sheer guts.

Say you're holding three of a kind. Your opponent, the wise guy, is taking one card on the draw. He has these possibilities against your threes. Higher three's and a kicker. (Chance to improve his hand, 11 to 1.) Maybe he's holding two pair. Only improvement could be a full house. Chances against his making it on a 1-card discard and draw, 7 to 1. He might be holding four cards of the same suit, trying for a flush. Odds against his making it are 4 to 1, or one chance in 5.

My advice, brother: sit tight, hold your sphincter muscle firmly, and hope the odds are working in your favor. In the long run they will.

Let's take an imaginary hand. Everyone has turned down except you and your opponent. You went in with three Jacks, discarded and drew two cards but failed to improve your hand. Now your opponent, who opened the hand in the first place, so you know he had to have at least a pair of Queens, (because YOU held three jacks) can only be going for a full house or four of a kind. A pair of queens puts him out of the running for a flush or a straight or a straight flush. Odds against his drawing one card and beating your three Jacks are like this:

Full house	12 to 1 against
4 of a kind	45 to 1

Of course, he might be holding three queens, but that's a decision you must make for yourself. No table of odds can tell you exactly what your opponent caught in the deal.

But let's suppose you've got a high set of cards. Unless your opponent were a comparative newcomer to the game of poker, and he were holding three of a kind, high, on the deal, he wouldn't draw a single card unless he'd slipped his trolley.

All things considered, however, three of any kind puts you in a strong bargaining position, and if they're decently high, eights or nines or better, you're perfectly justified and indeed would be foolish not to bet them down to the wire.

There are rules that allow for the use of "jokers" or other wild cards. This alters the chances of getting a better hand upward, but in no way affects the "bust probability, which is always 1-1.

As I don't consider these ladylike games poker, I refuse to discuss them.

A last word on the subject of odds and betting in poker: the draw is only *part* of the play. Every play by and every action by each participant in a poker game is significant. Some players would spend a hundred dollars in the course of a friendly game just for the pleasure (to them) of winning a ten dollar pot by bluffing. In other words, they're natural born bluffers, and relatively easy to spot after a half-hour or so of play. Others are very conservative, play by the book, and only bet when they have 'em. Watch these guys. If and when they run a bluff, the play it as they've played every other winning hand they've held. The size of the individual bet and the manner in which it's made will often clue you in. As a general rule, however, the highest hand wins almost every time, for few players will allow themselves to be bluffed out of a pot.

My final word. Learn by heart, so that it's almost automatic with you, the odds AGAINST making a certain type of hand. Watch the other fellow's discards.

And remember: play by the book, keep your wits and sanity about you, forget "hunches," ignore the bluffers, and above all, KNOW YOUR ODDS.

You'll win, in the long run.

In five card stud, the odds are the same, with your first card face down and the next four cards being dealt face up.

Odds, although they don't seem to, remain the same as in draw, except *there is no draw*. One down, four up, that's it.

Seven card stud is a different matter altogether. I play it pretty well, but I don't recommend it, nor would I attempt in the limited space of this book to set up the odds and possibilities of this game. They're practically infinite.

Besides all which, we're coming to my favorite card game pretty soon, the one you and I have been waiting to write about and read about. Blackjack, 21, call it what you will. Still the most fascinating game in the world today, one of the most "active" games (the money really moves in a hurry) and the next best house odds in a casino, except craps. It's simple, it's fun to play, and I can tell you *how to beat it!*

Chapter XXI

"MOST FUN AND PROFIT — 21"

Call me prejudiced, if you will. Or even call me stupid. I've been called worse. I know, my knowledge of odds tells me, that a player can make money more easily at the craps table than playing 21, yet this is so much my favorite game of all that I could (and probably will) expond on it at great length. It's a classic game in the sense that, in the long run, you're trying to beat the dealer, to outfigure him, and he's doing the same to you. It's a head-to-head game if you know your odds (very few people do) or how to make a correct play (fewer people know that).

Also, I always get a kick out of watching the others,

the various kinds of players. I've never dealt any of the games mentioned in this book. I'm a betting commissioner (unofficial, that is, not connected with the city, county or state, but rather with the guys who take or lay the odds).

So, in a very real sense, I play for the fun of it, and as it's no fun playing unless you're winning, I play to win, even if I don't need the money. I just like the game. And, as I say, I find myself staring with fascination at some of the other people who play it.

Surprisingly few of them know anything about the game of 21 at all, and still others have just a smattering or an understanding — these last often take the worst beating at the table. Who was it who once said "A little knowledge is a dangerous thing?"

I have seen a player hit a ten-four deal with an Ace, and turn his cards over thinking he was beat. When the dealer took the time to explain carefully to him that he hadn't gone bust because the Ace can count as either one or eleven this same player told the dealer, "Don't tell me how to play, I know this game!"

I saw another player, same type of breed, take a hit on an Ace, two and seven (twenty). She drew a five and now had fifteen. She stopped. After the play was over, the dealer, again patiently, told her she had hit a twenty. You'd think she would have said something like, "Oh, my God!" Instead, she told the dealer she was perfectly capable of counting, and that all he should do was deal the cards and keep quiet — that's what he was getting paid for.

Then, of course, there are the superstitious players, and there are a lot of them. Some men won't play at a table where a woman is playing. If one should walk up while he's playing, he'll just sort of squat down on his stool and not look in her direction trying, in effect, not to see the woman who had such unadulterated gall as to walk into "his" game.

There is a bit of reasoning behind this particular form of superstitution which, in all honesty, can't be denied. A bad player is very distracting to even an average player, let alone a good one. And women are quite notoriously pretty poor at 21.

And there are many other kinds of players, types which never fail to fascinate me. As a matter of fact, I can often just stand and chat with the pit boss, and just as often shake my head in amazement at some of the activity.

There is the restless player who never stays at any one table very long. There is the guy who is bored and plays only because he has nothing else to do. This one pays very little attention to the game. And this guy "bugs" both the dealer and the other players in the game by his complete lack of interest.

There is the character who won't go to an empty table because he doesn't want to play head-and-head with the dealer, although this is by far the best way to play 21. Here, no one else at the table can spoil *your* hand, and the dealer definitely doesn't have the best of it.

Then there's the overly happy cat who laughs out loud when he busts with a twenty-two or twenty-three, and giggles throughout the entire play. He also laughs at the misfortunes of others which makes him far from popular around the tables.

Also, there's a type I've come to call "the mumbler." He plays a very slow and deliberate game, always apparently trying to figure out the odds in his mind as he goes along, and compels all of the other players to wait while he thinks things over. I call him "the mumbler" mainly because he unconsciously moves his lips and sometimes even mumbles beneath his breath, to himself.

Still another of these annoying pest-type players is the one who keeps his chips in his pocket, so that nobody knows how he's doing. Generally, even he doesn't know.

I think you'll agree with me that it's fortunate that no dealer, at least not to my knowledge, has ever had to preside over a table at which all of these types were represented. If so, I'm sure the poor fellow would wind up in the looney bin.

There are some pretty nutty gamblers floating around the clubs and casinos, but thank God the average player is just another nice guy who's come to Las Vegas to see a show or two and win or lose a few dollars.

Now, here's something you might find difficult to believe. It pains a dealer to see some poor joker consistently do the wrong thing. Why this is, or why it should be true, I don't know, as the dealer's job is mainly to win as much money for the house as he possibly can. Yet, I've even seen a pit boss, unable to stand the sight of some poor man or woman simply giving their money away, and watched him walk over to them and quietly point out what he or she is doing wrong. Sometimes this kind-hearted soul will get thanked for his trouble and thoughtfulness, and sometimes he will get roundly cursed, because this player figures the dealer and/or the pit boss have him figured for a pigeon, and are simply trying to win his money a little faster.

Yes, human nature being what it is, I would compare the game of 21 to heavy drinking. Over a period of time it will bring out the best or the worst in an individual.

Let's explain this game of Blackjack — or "21" — as it is played in a casino or gambling club in Nevada.

It's not quite like the game you play at home, although the rules are basically the same. The dealer shuffles the cards and deals a round to as many players (see layout) up to six as there may be in the game. He also deals himself a card. Now he deals around again, including himself once more. The only difference is that both of your cards are face down, while his second card is face up so that you know at least half of his hand, while he obviously knows nothing of yours.

Bets must be placed in front of each player before even the first card is dealt. In all clubs the player goes first and can either draw, if he wants to, or simply look at his hand, place it face down, and put his money on top of it signifying that he doesn't wish any more cards.

A standard rule in Nevada allows players, when they want to be hit, to gently scrape the cards on the cloth, toward them. When they do not want to be hit, they slid their cards under their money. Object of the game, of course, is for the player to hit an even 21, or as close to it as he can without "going over" that number. If he busts, he merely turns his card face up.

There is little, or no need for conversation at a 21

table and you're far better off if you keep your mouth shut.

The dealer is the last person to play, and he must hit sixteen or stand on any "hard" seventeen. The player, naturally, may stop at any time he wishes. I bring this point up because there are all sorts of other rules in games played at home. For example, if you get a Blackjack in a home game (which is any ten or face card plus an Ace) it's customary to pass the deal to the player who got the Blackjack. In a casino, if you get a blackjack, you immediately turn it over and receive three to two for your bet, but you never get the deal. The house always retains the deal as the game goes on its merry way.

I've heard it said that 21 is just a game of luck, that there is no skill involved. Nuts! In 21 a player who knows his odds, has some degree of skill, and a knowledge of how to handle his money, will win. I make this statement categorically.

The other players will lose.

You see, it's the average player's theory that when he loses it's bad luck, but when he wins it's skill. Show me a person who tells you that 21 is a game of luck and I'll show you a loser.

It's an old game, dating from way back in the 1300's. Its symbolism, supposedly, is built around the attainment of adulthood, at the traditional age of 21. The equality of the suits, supposedly, was the symbol of the equality of the members of the family. This is a random thing that I've read somewhere during the past, and I pass it along to you for what it might be worth — which, I don't suppose is very much.

It would seem to me that 21, as a game of cards, was almost inevitable because it comes so close to being a perfect balance of luck, skill and money management. The latter two are the most important elements involved, so that you really have a 2 to 1 edge over pure chance in this particular game. Luck enters into the play (if you're a skilled player to begin with) if you're fortunate enough to sit down during a dealer's bad streak. Oh, yes, the dealer is playing the same game you are, and he, too, can have a bad run of cards. When this happens, and you're astute enough to recognize it, take full advantage of it. No one's going to blame you, least of all the dealer, or the house. If the dealers hands, contrariwise, are running hot, astute money management will enable you, with your skill, to ride it out with a minimum of losses.

On almost every hand dealt, you have to meet a challenge and make a correct decision. "Should I stop, or should I hit?" When all of your decisions are correct, you are a good player.

There's a right way to play, and there's a wrong way to play every hand. In addition, there's a little thing called intestinal fortitude, or to put it more plainly, "guts." Now, each and all individuals in a game of chance has a different conception of what a "big" bet is, and this, of course, is based upon the size of his individual bankroll.

For example, if the laws of chance which govern, to a great extent, the game of 21, call for you to take a hit, and you're only playing the house minimum it doesn't take too much guts to take that hit. But let's suppose you have ten or even twenty-five bucks bet on the same hand, and it's really going to cut into your bankroll if you lose, — do you take a hit or don't you? This is where guts comes into play because if the law of averages works for a $1 bettor it will work just the same for the higher priced bettor. It's your decision to make, of course, but it's the all-important decision — the one that separates the men from the boys — and the pigeons from the tigers. In this case, or example I just mentioned, there's only one thing to do, only one correct play to make. *You must take that hit!*

In other words, you can't have guts only up to a certain figure and expect to win at 21. If you ask me, "Do you mean you must play consistently, always, no matter the amount of the bet?" the answer is not only simple, but also obvious. If a play is right, it's right, no matter how much the amount of money involved. If it's wrong, it's always wrong, no matter how much, or how little, money is involved.

One final word of advice on the game of 21, before we get into the actual play, and it's the same rule that applies to all games of chance. When you're losing, more or less consistently, bet low, and *don't chase your dollars!*

The world always turns, and so does your luck. When it does, start betting high again. And, if you study the game and follow the instructions I give you — to the letter — memorize them so that you have eliminated all guess work, you'll find it easier to play with confidence and to expect as well as to be able to handle losing streaks. It's the pressure of losing that quite often will make you pile up mistake upon mistake until you've managed to compound a felony against yourself. You'll get in so deep that you can't possibly get out winners, even if your luck changes for the better.

Above all, don't watch the other player or his action; because a guy has a big pile of chips in front of him and looks like a confident big-money gambler, it ain't necessarily so. Those guys are often brilliant men who have made lots of money in their own field, such as oil wells or undertaking, or ladies garments. And they often play 21 like jerks, making mistake after mistake while the newcomer to the game thinks to himself, "I'll follow this fellow's way of playing. After all, look at all the money he's got stacked up in front of him." All the while, he probably knows less about the game than the poor chumps who try to emulate his mistakes.

Chapter XXII

"OF ALL GAMES — WHY PLAY 21?"

This is a question that I've often been asked, and, while I have a sort of answer for it, I am sure there are many more subconscious drives at work which — between them — form the almost irressistible impulses to win or lose (and it doesn't really matter) at this rather particular game, for its many fans, followers and what you might term "radical" players who wouldn't think of winning or losing — or even wasting their time — at any other form of gambling.

My theory, such as it is, goes something like this: In no other game is the player so closely associated with the dealer. He's the guy you have to outsmart in order to win. Now I must add something to this latter statement.

When more than one player sits around the board it's needful, necessary, and even imperative that they watch the play of the others who are also bucking the house with them.

I realize that I contradict myself here — in a sense. First, as in the chapter just past, I advised that you should, to a greater or lesser extent, ignore the other players at the table — a game between you and the dealer.

And, so you should.

But what you must *also do,* as opposed to what you probably will do, is a different kettle of fish entirely. If you have to think about that for a moment, go right ahead. Be my guest. It will help you learn the game!

Human nature, being what it is, no one, even the roughest, toughest player of them all can say without abusing the truth, "I've never let my impulses get ahead of my knowledge of odds and percentages. I never will. I always know the one right play to make at any given time."

I won't call the speaker who makes this all embracing statement a liar, but I must say he has to be stretching a point — or two!

Additionally, there's another facet to this popular — possibly the most popular — card game.

For example, there are a dozen or more dealers in Las Vegas whom I can beat consistently. After all, a dealer is only a human being, as are you and me. He has a set of certain rules for playing, which he must follow. He has a better than average knowledge of

DEALER MUST DRAW TO
INSURANCE PAYS 2-1
INSURANCE PAYS 2-1

16 AND STAND ON ALL 17's
INSURANCE PAYS 2-1

the game because he spends eight hours a day, or night, playing it — watching the action of all sorts and all types of players, from the tough gambler to the tender pigeon.

Still, he's only a human, as I said above. If he has a failing at all (and most dealers, as humans, do) it's in abiding by the rules set down by the casino to the point where his play is almost one hundred percent automatic, and nothing of the personal element is allowed to enter into it, unless he suspects there is a cheater at his table.

Now, I want to explain a strange thing to you; as a player, if you are channelled in the right direction, and know your odds, as well as being completely oriented as to the proper procedures of play, the greater your chances are of walking away from that table as a winner. You see, the odds do not favor the dealer so much that he can disregard the other four or five players sitting at the table with you. While he's playing each one of them, including you, he must play individually, but you're playing *only* against him.

There are figures which guarantee the dealer (unless he should fall asleep at the switch) a percentage in his favor, and the house expects him to make either this percentage — or a better one — night after night and week after week, or he will speedily be entered into the ranks of the unemployed.

Of course, about the only way this can happen to him is for him to start playing his own game — like a "player."

I know tables in Las Vegas where the dealer can give you an "automatic 18" on each and every hand,

and still wind up grinding you down to your case dollar.

As I've mentioned before, there are things you should do as well as things you shouldn't do in a 21 game. In my next chapter, I'll try to go into them a little more explicitly, with actual facts and figures. I think both the facts and figures will surprise you, perhaps even startle you, and maybe even amaze you.

If you follow my instructions to the letter, you should and must win. You cannot lose, because, actually, no matter what you may read or hear to the contrary, if you play the same kind of game as the dealer, you must win.

The casino doesn't really care if you win or lose, in fact, the management likes to see a winner at every table. First, it's good advertising, and secondly, there's always another poor, ignorant pigeon, knowing very little about the game, and nothing at all about the odds involved, sitting there waiting to slide onto your "lucky" stool as soon as you've picked up your winning checks and leave the table to cash them in.

You see, the house hasn't lost anything because the action is still at the table. In five out of six — make that ninety out of a hundred — 21 players have only a superficial knowledge of the game. These are the boys on whom the casino makes their profit.

Now what can be made out of all the things we've discussed so far?

First, there's nothing mechanical about the game. The guy deals you a few cards, and deals himself a few cards. Unless there is an absolute and utter jerk at the table, there will be little, hopefully no conversation, so it's a relatively quiet game, a game on which a good player can concentrate. Unlike the craps table, with two dealers, a stickman, and ten to twenty players, all calling loudly for some kind of idiot bet, and all of whom can tend to confuse you, especially if you happen to be a newcomer to the gaming tables, 21 is a quiet, unmechanical game which pits your knowledge of cards and odds against that of the dealers.

All of the above is the way I, personally, see this game, and explain its fascination for young and old, rich and poor, male and female.

There are, undoubtedly, many other reasons for the popularity of 21, some of them, perhaps, more valid than mine. If I'm not correct in my many years of playing, and of observing other players, then I must most humbly apologize. Yet, it seems to me that there is a great deal of reason on my side.

First, there are certain things — certain rules — by which the dealers must abide, rules and reasons which in no way can affect you. You play your game in any method, manner or way you so desire. You don't, for example, *have* to hit a sixteen nor stand on a seventeen. This, as I've explained, your dealer *must* do. So, here you are given an edge, perhaps a slight one, but definitely an edge over the dealer. I've mentioned this before, and I am mentioning it once more to make sure you don't forget it. You, as a player, are in effect at all times playing man-to-man, head-to-head, against that one dealer. He, on the contrary, is playing not only you, but two, three, four or five other players. As a general rule, if he collects three out of five hands, he's grinding out the good old house PC.

This is what he was hired for. And this is the only

thing in which he is interested.

If you've ever played Blackjack in a friendly game, or even at home, you know from experience that the dealer has the best of it for just the same reason. There's really very little difference between the game of Blackjack in your own home and the game of 21 as played in a casino. Odds are about the same, except that in your casinos the odds are slightly more in favor of the player.

One of the most fatal mistakes for a dealer to make is to so dislike the style of play of one specific individual at his table that he plays this person rather than his percentages. This is something that happens really more often than you might imagine because dealers (and I know I'm repeating myself, but feel it necessary) are not only human, but spend eight hours daily being either humiliated, bugged, cheated (or attempts to do so) and insulted, so that their patience does tend to wear more than a little bit thin.

It is also the reason for the frequency of their several "rest periods" during each shift. These give them a chance to get up, move around a bit, take a breath of fresh air and see what the other boys are doing. And, not so incidentally, hope and pray that the maggot at the table will have moved on to some other table, or some other form of gambling. Let him make some other dealer unhappy.

A small hint: A good time to hit a 21 table is about an hour before the end of the dealer's shift when all he wants to do is get that last hour out of the way, collect his pay, have a drink or two, and go home to sob on his wife's shoulder. During that last hour of his shift, the pickings are just a tiny bit easier.

I feel like a rat-fink for telling you this, but it's the honest-to-God truth.

Take it, and make of it what you will.

FLASH! I just got word — as I was writing this chapter — from the new racetrack and its first day in action in Las Vegas. As I told you, I'm not really a believer in this thing, and probably never will be. There was a vast turnout of 3,852 people in the newly renovated backyard baby Thunderbird Downs at the first days opening in its attempt to restore horse-racing to Vegas. It was an admittably pint-sized turn-out which appeared more important to the Godfathers of this proposed week-end track; President Joe Wells and Race Secretary Richard Thompson than to this reporter.

Opening day saw a field of ten races, five quarter-horse and five thoroughbred displays to a total handle of $61,478.00. The figure included a daily double, "big six" and a quinella on the last race. Losses for the first day — so far as the promoters were concerned — were $10,000.00. It's reported that the handful of spectators enjoyed the carnival atmosphere, and the fast action on the ⅜th mile track, with it's 540 yard straightaway for quarter horses. There was one winning ticket in the "big six" worth $2,968.00. The winner's name was not disclosed.

I just threw that in so that you don't think I'm not keeping you posted and up to date on the current events in Vegas. Now, let's get back to our discussion on 21, or Blackjack.

Well, let's postpone it for a minute, come to think about it. I have a strange feeling that you're about ready for some facts rather than my possibly poor theories on the game.

We'll try that in the upcoming chapter.

Meanwhile, memorize these numbers:

7-8-9-10-Ace.

That's not so hard to do is it?

7-8-9-10-Ace.

Remember them. They, together with another sequence of the same or approximately the same length, can make you or break you in that wonderful, wacky, *profitable* game of "21."

7-8-9-10-Ace.

Chapter XXIII

"HOW TO HIT WITHOUT OVERPLAYING"

Wouldn't it be wonderful if I could lay down a set of flat laws which would enable you to do just that? Hit, without busting?

Well, I can't and neither can any man walking, past present or, presumably future. If and when such a person comes along, doling out such advice, you may be sure that "21" tables will disappear from the face of the Earth.

I've often heard the remark made (and so, presumambly, have you) "I can always win when I get good cards."

Who can't?

Lots of people can't, to tell you the honest truth, because they don't know good cards when they see them. If the object of the game is to come as close to the figure 21 as you can without going over, and closer to it than the dealer, and you draw, say, a pair of Kings (20) on the deal, you'd be kind of nutty to hit it.

I bet you can't even remember that sequence of numbers I gave you in the very last chapter. Let's revue them, and show you exactly where they fit into the play.

The numbers I gave you were 7-8-9-10 or Ace.

7-8-9-10 or Ace.

Now take another sequence of numbers, which are easier to remember. Start with the 12, and read up. 12-13-14-15 or 16.

In all honesty if you draw one of these hands on the deal, it's a lousy hand, what's called a "breaking" hand or a stiff. Now, if the dealer (see where these sequences come into play?) has a 7-8-9-10 or Ace showing, you MUST hit your lousy hand. Even if you get this combination from more than one card, it doesn't make any difference. Hit it.

Many things can happen, but you're staying on an even keel with the dealer, playing it not only the way he'd play it but the way he *MUST* play it (see layout).

You may have, for instance, a seven and five on the deal, which is twelve and a nowhere number. You must hit it, especially if the dealer's "up" card runs from 7 through Ace. You hit your twelve, and get a four. That's sixteen. *HIT IT AGAIN*. No matter what you think, no matter how you feel, *HIT IT AGAIN!*

In other words, you must HIT these breaking hands until you have seventeen or better. Don't be afraid to hit such a hand against the dealer's up card showing 7 through Ace. You can't hurt yourself, and if you *DON'T* hit you *CAN'T* win. If you hit, you have just a good a chance as the dealer, which is about all you can ask for, right?

Any boob can sit tight on a twenty and have a reasonable chance (better than even) of winning. That's not playing "21," though, that's just being lucky, and while I'm the last guy in the world to knock a hatfull of good, old-fashioned luck, it's a commodity you can't count on having at all times. Or even most of the time. Just sometimes. The rest of the time, it's you and the dealer, each knowing the odds, outdrawing and out-thinking each other.

I've been told by some fairly consistent (once or twice a week) players "You gotta admit it takes a lot of guts to hit a 15 or 16 when the dealer has only a 7 or 8 up."

Believe me, when you know the game it takes a lot more nerve *NOT* to hit under those circumstances.

And hit when you have to. Don't let the size of the bet make you sweat. Hit when the "book" calls for a hit. The money isn't anyone's permanent property, anyway — not as long as you're still in action. It's just been moved from one side of the table to the other, and it can move back to your side just as easily as it moved to the dealer's side.

Remember those sequences of numbers once again.

7 through Ace showing on dealers up card.

12 through 16 in your hand.

TAKE A HIT.

Here's a happier sequence: Let's take your "stiff hand" as just mentioned, 12 through 16.

Now, if the dealer's *up* card is one of these: 2, 3, 4, 5 or 6, just slide your cards under your money, which means you're through betting. Let *HIM* sweat this one.

Hit all breaking hands when the dealer shows 7 through Ace.

Stop betting immediately if the dealer shows 2, 3, 4, 5 or six.

That doesn't take a lot of concentration, but it takes a lot of willpower.

This gives you a chance to win and makes the game more enjoyable. There are refinements, and we'll get into those, but these are BASICS. Without them, you're just going to have a miserable time at the 21 tables, and after all, you don't have to leave home and come to Vegas to be miserable, do you?

I've sen any number of players who know nothing of the stopping and/or hitting sequences outlined above, who'll knock their brains out trying to make a decision as to the right or wrong way to play. Couple of hands later, the identical situation will arise, and they'll do exactly the opposite, hoping (I presume) that there must be *some* correct way to play a hand). There is, and I've just given it to you. It's so simple, it's like the paper clip. A guy will say: "Now, *I* should have thought of that myself!"

There's a moral there, and I'm going to pass it along.

There's a time and a place for everything, as you know. There is no such thing as making a play in 21 that doesn't have a reason, no real meaning. You're trying to beat the dealer and the odds. He's on exactly the same kick.

You hit for a certain reason, or you play them as they were dealt for a certain reason, but there are a lot more odds you should learn and retain for future use.

Splitting Pairs

Here's a phase of the game, not governed by strict rules so far as the house is concerned, but which must be governed by strict rules so far as you, the player, are concerned.

A twenty is difficult to obtain on the two-card "deal," and I don't really care what you think you see. The odds are almost 9 to 1 against your getting a twenty in your first two cards. Not so easy, is it? And the odds are much higher against your drawing a pair of fives, fours or nines. They're good hands, so why split them?

Now, you split like this: you're dealt two cards, as are all the other players, and as the dealer does to himself. Only he has one card showing. When you split a pair, you turn them face up, place an equal bet on the second card. Then the dealer deals to you face down. You can draw as many cards to each of yours as you need, you're just playing two hands.

Some players, not knowing the game, will split a pair of eights against any card the dealer has up, *hoping* the dealer has a small card underneath his hand. This is pure guesswork, and that's what we're trying to eliminate from the game. It's sort of like betting into a high card with the worst of it. Why risk your money to find out if you've guessed properly? Even if you won, it would still be a lousy bet, and put you at the mercy of the dealer in future hands, as he'll immediately know you don't really understand the game.

So if you have a pair of eights, and the dealer is showing 8 through 10 up, just hit your sixteen, but don't split them.

It's a bad hand, but you might make it into a good hand. If you lose, you're only losing one hand instead of two.

But — you do and should split eights against a dealer's 2 through 7. Sevens are also a good hand to split against a dealer's 2 through 7, because 14 is a stiff or bad hand, and by splitting you are playing two hands, seven each, and there are 32 ways to improve these such as 1 out of 16 pictures, which will give you seventeen, one of 4 Aces, which will give you 18, a two, three or four which will give you nine, ten or eleven, which in turn will give you an opportunity to draw a high card for a winning hand.

You split sixes against the dealers 5; and only against the dealers 5, because there are only five cards that can help your hand after you split.

When the dealer has a five up, he is at his biggest disadvantage in the game. You are at your best advantage. Don't make me explain this in detail, because, while I can, I'd have to go into such a lengthy and confusing table of odds it would be of no help. Just do as I say in this instance, and you'll have the advantage over the dealers, odds-wise, whenever such a situation arises.

Actually, it all boils down to the fact that the dealer has more ways of helping his hand when he has only a small card up than the player who splits sixes against the small card.

When the dealer has a deuce or three showing, this is very dangerous for the player who's split his sixes, because he's at the wrong end of the bargain. Don't take the worst of it.

When you step inside a casino, you've got the worst of it even before you make a bet. Just try to remember "don't split sixes against any card other than the five."

Now when the dealer has a 2 through 7 showing, split two's and three's because your chances of improving your hand are at least as good as the dealers. The dealer, remember, must hit on sixteen or less. But you don't have to.

Splitting Aces is a must, no matter what the dealer has showing. Remember, in most clubs, you receive only one card on each Ace. You might receive two low cards, thereby have two lousy hands. There's nothing you can do about this unfortunately, but it is still to your advantage, over the long run, to split aces. The odds are better than two to one against your receiving a ten, or a picture card, in one play; but don't forget, you don't have to have 21 to win.

You can also receive a 7, 8 or 9. Here, the percentage is a little bit in your favor. You can have a stopping hand after being hit with one card. So, continue to split Aces. It's the best pair to split because, again, and finally, it puts the odds in your favor.

If you'll follow these rules I've outlined, on splitting pairs, you'll not get into any trouble, nor will you lose money by making a wrong split against the dealers up card.

Many players will split a pair, regardless of what the dealer is showing, which gives them about as much chance of winning as a soap bubble in a meat-grinder!

It might be wise to practice your rules in a club with the lowest possible of the minimum bets — say, 25¢. In this way, your education will be just as complete, but won't cost you nearly as much in the way of "tuition fees."

"Down for Double"

A lot of people who visit the tables fairly regularly, don't even know what this means. They should, but they don't. It's quite simple to explain. Let's say you're betting the house minimum, which is probably $1. You are then dealt two cards, which total eleven. You turn your cards up, and add one more dollar to the $1 you've already bet. In other words, what you're trying to do is double your money, and the dealer will now throw you one card — face down. Sounds simple enough to you, doesn't it?

Here are the correct and incorrect ways to make this bet. *ALWAYS* go down for double on your two card combination of ten or eleven, when the dealer has a two, three, four, five, six, seven or eight showing. NEVER double down when the dealer has a nine, ten or Ace showing. And never go down for double if your own combination is less than ten or eleven.

Many times you get stuck by going down for this double with what might have been a good hitting hand.

All you can do at that point, is to pray that the dealer will "bust." Praying has never seemed to help much in a casino — you must "PLAY," not "pray."

Some players will go down for double with only twelve or thirteen in their hand, and it often makes one wonder where they get their money, or how they keep enough of it to continue playing for more than a minimum length of time.

Even a good player is fairly gullible, and is overly-trusting when gambling. They all hope that any advice will help them win. They might as well forget it! If you can remember the few simple rules I've given you thus far, you don't need any more outside advice in order to make a good showing at the tables, and if you can't remember these simple rules, you shouldn't be gambling in the first place.

I note that some of the clubs are now offering "free instructions on how to gamble" during the morning hours. In other words, they give you a stack of special chips and let you play and call attention to your mistakes, explain the rules of the game, and so on.

Hooray for them!

I guarantee you that no casino is going to give you information such as that contained in this little book. This would be much like a super-market calling you and saying "don't buy the lettuce today because we're cutting the price by half tomorrow!"

No casino I've ever heard of is operating for anything other than profit.

A word or two of final advice to you, and then I'm goin to conclude my lecture on this, my favorite game, by discussing the most confusing of all the cards in the deck.

1. Always split Aces.
2. Hit all "soft" hands, from soft thirteen to soft seventeen, regardless of what the dealer has showing.
3. Hit all your breaking hands from twelve to sixteen when the dealer has a 7, 8, 9, 10, or picture or Ace face up.
4. Don't hit your breaking, or bad, hand from twelve to sixteen when the dealer has a 2, 3, 4, 5, 6 face up.
5. Always bet more when winning, less when losing.
6. Most important of all, study and practice and play — this way — always. There is only one right way to play any game, and in the overall picture, it's naturally going to be the best way.

"Most Confusing Card in the Deck"

Unquestionably, the Ace in this game of 21, is the card that confuses more people, and leads them into making more misplays, bad plays and mistakes, than any other card, or even any other combination of cards in the deck.

This, no doubt, is because the Ace counts for either one or eleven. Thus, when you're holding, let's say a four and an Ace in your first two cards, you're holding what is called a "soft hand." It could be played as either five, or fifteen, and for some reason, a player can develop a mental block whenever he receives one of these Aces, either in the deal or the draw. And yet, the Ace can weigh most heavily in your favor if played properly.

For example. You receive anything from a two through a six, plus an Ace. If you receive any one of these two card combinations on a deal, you should count the Ace as eleven. Two and Ace are thirteen, three and Ace are fourteen, and so on right up to the Ace, six. Hit these hands all the time, regardless of what the dealer has showing. They're not what you'd necessarily call good hands, but by hitting them you are receiving a free card — in a manner of speaking — because you cannot go over when you ask for the first hit. However, if you receive a good card, your hand can be improved. In other words, "you can hit it, but you can't hurt it."

I have seen any number of players stop on a soft sixteen. You might as well hand your money to the dealer, if you're going to do this. I've asked other players why they stopped on a soft seventeen, and invariably get the reply, "Why spoil a seventeen?"

What's so good about a soft seventeen? It's a bad hand, and how can you spoil something already rotten? Some players will draw an Ace and three in two cards, which is a soft fourteen, then hit it with a seven, which makes 21. But, players will still hit. They either can't think well under pressure, or can't add under any circumstances. You can't quite explain any of this to a person while they are actually playing the game, so I hope you'll take heed of it now.

Here are a few more simple rules you should follow and facts you should try to remember when you play the game called 21.

Anything up through a sixteen is a lousy hand, and it should be hit (with the exceptions I've mentioned earlier).

A seventeen is a poor hand, even if the dealer must stand on seventeen.

An eighteen is a fair hand.

Nineteen and twenty are good hands.

Blackjack — or 21 — can't be beat.

Above all, use your good common sense while you're playing the game. It's the one game which gives you an even break, or possibly even a small edge over it's dealer, if you know the rules of the game, how to manage your money, the laws of odds and averages, and play it that way. And that way only!

Here's just one more thing about blackjack I'll bet many of you didn't know. When you sit down at the 21 table to make a bet, you place your money in a square box, about 4" by 4" marked off on the table (see diagram). Directly in front of this square, *in some clubs,* is a smaller box, and in this box are the words "Insurance — 2 to 1." In clubs that don't have this insurance box, the insurance bet is placed directly in front of the box in which you made your original bet. This means when the dealer has an Ace showing, he'll say "does anyone care for insurance?" What he means is that he will bet you — or lay you the odds of 2 to 1 — that he does *not* have a ten or picture card in the hole. If you think he has that picture card or ten in the hole, the rules allow you to put up half of the amount of your original bet in the insurance box. If he does have the ten or picture there, he has a blackjack. If you had taken insurance, you would then have a standoff or a push. In other words, you have just what you started with.

Most players that take insurance don't really understand they are playing with their own money. You either break even, or lose half of your original bet.

Much as it hurts me to say this, don't take insurance.

In conclusion, in 21, as in all other gambling games, you must give your money and yourself a chance to win. There's only one answer to this — one I've told you at least twenty-five times so far through this book: Start small, according to your original bankroll, increase your bets only when you win, and are playing with the casino's money. Never bet less if you're winning. Never bet more if you're losing.

And lots of luck. I hope and believe that this book will be worth its weight in gold to you, or at any rate, in silver dollars!

Chapter XXIV

"MISH-MASH"

Naturally, it is impossible for one person to put everything they know about gambling into any one book, and you will always remember later a great many things that either could, or should have been included in it. So, I'm using my last few pages to sort of try to clean up some of the odds and ends that have occurred to me after re-reading the first twenty-three chapters.

I will make absolutely no attempt to set them into any particular order, but I know there are a lot of things you'd like to know about one or another of the principal gambling games — things I may have failed to cover for you. For example, I've heard rumors about there being "systems" of beating various games of chance. They are supposed to be absolutely unbeatable — so perfect, in fact, that their originators are barred from all and any casinos in Nevada. To this, I can only reply, "nonsense."

Any man with money in his pocket is welcome to come up to Vegas, come into any casino and try his system whenever he wishes. The club will even furnish him with a comfortable stool, a pad of paper and a pencil. I've watched many of these system players in action, and while I have no doubts as to their honesty, and belief in the worthwhile society of their own communities, there is no system I've yet seen, nor in my humble opinion, can there be a system evolved to beat the laws of both chance and average. (Ask any insurance company).

Another question I've been asked, is do I beileve in a thing called "beginner's luck." The answer is a flat no. For every beginner who has managed to make a killing that first time around, there are another thousand or more — the ones you never read about — who can consider themselves "lucky" they got out of town with their shirts. Give me a casino full of nothing but beginners, especially if they're loaded with loot, and I'll show you one of the biggest profit days in the history of the operation itself, for while a beginner may have a streak of luck, he often doesn't recognize it for what it is, and often, even if he does, doesn't know enough about the game itself to take any advantage of his good fortune.

Some people want to know exactly what I mean by

the word "shill." A shill is a man or woman, paid by the house to sit in on a game which would, without them, be empty. They are used because so many players hesitate to start their game at an empty table. The shill makes bets, and otherwise acts as a come-on, but when the table starts to fill up, he'll get up and move on to another table where his (or her) action is more urgently required. I, personally, see nothing wrong in this as it can cost you, the player, not one red penny.

In other words, the shill is just a kind of window-dressing supplied by the management to make you, his customer, feel more at ease.

When I was discussing horse-racing, earlier in the book, I forgot to give you a few short cuts, and in so doing, bad-rapped the selections that appear in the daily newspapers. As I said, and must repeat, I know of no one handicapper who shows a profit at the end of a racing meet, however there's always one who has done better than all of the others. Keep your eye on him, and notice if he does better at certain distances, and with different purses. Then, follow him for the picks in these races. I will caution you on one thing. If you intend to win (or try to win) money at the track, you should know the history of every horse, and every jockey as well as having a good head for figures. Sounds simple. Believe me, it isn't.

Another thing I've ben asked is can I "guarantee" my method of playing various games of chance? Of course not. I can only guarantee that you'll last longer in a game, and have a better chance of winning if you follow these methods of play.

Also, I would appreciate your understanding that —

by necessity — I have tried to keep these methods inso-far as this book is concerned, to the very minimum of explanations so that you won't be confused by too many decimal points — decimal points which, after you've been gaming regularly and for comparatively high stakes — can make a tremendous difference in the course of your evening. I tried to write this without what we would call "refinements" in other words, my idea was to teach you to bake a cake, not cover it with icing for you.

Is it true that the more money you have the easier it is to win? No. Absolutely not. I have seen more than my share of players with plenty of money. And I've seen them get hooked, get in so far chasing their money that they had no chance at all. You can be a tough gambler with a short bankroll, believe me.

The limit always stops the really big bettors, and you'll very rarely see the casino take the limit off a game. The club's simply don't need that kind of business. They make it good enough with the many small players around. They can't hurt the clubs too much if they hit heavy, so most clubs have their limit, and they stick to it. The regular PC is a good enough living for them.

I also recall telling you that if you split Aces in the game of 21, you will receive only one card on each. This is not always true, as a few clubs in the event of your receiving another Ace for your "down card" will allow you to split it also. This, however, happens so rarely, it hardly seemed worth mentioning earlier. But, it does happen.

The limits on all clubs in Vegas, as well as throughout Nevada are quite different, no matter what you may hear otherwise. Every club has its own rules and its own limits on its games. The limit of the games are determined by the club owners, so whenever you read, or hear about someone betting five thousand dollars all in one lump sum, listen politely to the story, then file it away in your mental waste basket. It just doesn't happen. Once in a great, great while an owner will take off the limit for a heavy loser who also has plenty of cash left to lose. Even that doesn't happen much anymore.

"How long should I play at a table" is often asked.

Just as long as you're reasonably alert. When you get physically and mentally tired, when you have to stop and think for a moment before deciding what action to take in any given situation, you've had it for the time being. A walk and a cup of coffee is recommended if the cards or dice have been running well for you, otherwise, get some eggs, toast and coffee and hit the sack for a pleasant rest, thinking of how much ahead you're going to be when you wake up.

Don't let your money control you. You control your money. I've heard many players remark "One more bet, then I'm going to knock off for the day." They generally make that last bet a big one. Then he'll stay to recoup his loss (chasing his money) and wind up dropping his whole bundle.

When does a player leave a game a winner?

A player should bet according to the amount of money he came into the club with. The sooner he gets into the Casino's money, the better off he is, naturally. Let's say you come into a club with a couple of hundred dollars, and run it up to three or four hundred bucks, then start to lose a few hands.

Quit.

You're a winner, and you're chasing bad money if you hang around, which is the shortest short-cut to financial disaster I know of.

It's difficult, of course to know when to quit, and it's a decision you must make by yourself. I'll tell you this, though: play according to your original bankroll, and when you win enough, and start to lose a little, run like a bandit!

Just remember this: you might get a lot of free advice, but no refunds. No one is going to give back your losses to you. And don't wait, if you're a winner, to lose only until you are even with what you started with. Hell, why play at all if all you hope to do is lose or break even? It's a complete waste of time.

Let's see, what else?

I've said to not be afraid to ask a houseman or a dealer a question if you're ignorant of the game, and I mean it and meant it. Yet, I've had people tell me that they've done this and never got an answer. Well, you probably asked a real stupid question, and a dealer, like a bartender, develops a tin ear, a sort of mental device that screens out questions that make no sense, or questions that shouldn't be answered at that particular time because of the type of action around the table. Don't blame the dealer when this happens — blame yourself.

Another question, when do you stop if you're losing? That's up to you. Once you start, it's a sled ride, and that's downhill, you know. Best thing to do is quit when you've lost only a little, come back when the table is hotter.

Another question I've heard asked and been asked is "Doesn't the dealer ever make a mistake?" Dealers are only human, and humans can make a mistake. Dealers move from one casino to another, as an example, and will quote you the wrong rules automatically, especially if they're near the end of their shift and playing almost automatically. You're free to call the dealer on a bad call, or ask to see the pit boss. He's there to see you get a fair rattle, just as he's trying to watch out for the house interests, too.

Are dealers who lose more or less consistently, often fired? Quite often. The boss expects you to keep that PC coming his way.

Are the so-called *"BIG"* gamblers superstitious? Lord, yes! The stories I could tell about their superstitions would fill a book. One I know won't play if it's raining. Another won't change socks, shoes or even underwear, won't clean his fingernails, shave, wash or anything while he's on a winning streak, if it's even for so long as a month. I know another who will never wear a shirt again — he throws it away — if he's had a losing streak while wearing it.

There are many such superstitions.

Do these superstitions really affect the player concerned? Of course. This may be purely psychological, but if you've made up your mind that to do so and so will help you win, you'll go into the game feeling like a winner, and quite possibly win. If you think such-and-such will make you lose, you go into a game an automatic loser.

About horses, here's a frequently misunderstood thing that happens occasionally: you're betting on a horse to win in, say, an 8-horse field, and he finishes in a dead heat to win with another horse. What happens? Do you win, or what? You win, all right, but not as much as if he'd won all by himself.

The legal age limit to play in a Casino is 21, both men and women. Minors are strictly not allowed to gamble in any way, shape or form, so if you're a young-looking 22 or 23, don't be offended if a houseman politely asks to see your identification. That's his job, or part of it, and the Casino, understandably, doesn't feel like losing the license to stay open over any one player.

A couple of more and we'll call it a day.

Some people use foreign coins in the slot machines. This is against the law and carries a penalty of fine and a jail sentence or both. Don't risk it. It isn't worth it, anyway.

"Why," (and even the publisher asked me this question), "if you know so much about winning procedures, do you bother to write a book, or even work one way or another in the business? Why not just gamble for a living?"

No thank you. Let me put it this way. I don't have the nervous system of the true gambler. Pressure wears me out.

I will point out that you don't have to lay an egg, however, to know a good one. Even the dumbest person in the world knows more about eggs than the smartest chicken.

I like to play, and I do play, but never when it hurts

me should I lose. I'm no memory expert, no mental genius. My line of work is more on the idea of ascertaining certain facts, assembling them, then make odds on things happening one way or another. I never have to say "This one MUST win" or "That one MUST lose." I simply figure out the best probability, and make the odds on it accordingly.

I seldom lose at a gaming table, to tell you the truth, but then it isn't a way of life with me, either.

Most of the players who come to Las Vegas are reasonably uneducated in the rudiments of gambling, let alone the rules of the game, the odds, the laws of averages, the right and wrong way to play. The Casinos are aware of this. They're fairly fat and perhaps too complacent.

I think it's easier than ever to win, especially if you have a little knowledge of the game you're playing. If you have no such knowledge, you're a dead pigeon.

Try it my way. Practice at home if you like.

Take your next vacation in Las Vegas with the firm determination to see a few good shows, sleep well and comfortably, enjoy good food and come home with money in your pockets, preferably *winning* money. Now, get in there and pitch!

Chapter XXV

"OUTSIDE MONEY"

One thing we need badly in the State of Nevada is a lot more publicity (and I hope even this little book helps) about the strict manner in which we control our gambling.

There's been a lot of talk and a lot of phony stuff in the newspapers about "outside money" and "outside influence" at work in Nevada.

One of these has been a strong and persistent attempt to make much of the fact that funds from the Teamster's Union are invested here. Let me point out something:

1. The Teamster's Union is not, so far as I know, an unAmerican group. It's a union of truck drivers, and has various funds at its disposal to further its welfare and benefits program. I personally do not give a damn, one way or the other, but I fail to see how that union's funds, investment-wise, unless it was for trafficking in narcotics or white slavery, is of any concern. *Any such funds invested in Las Vegas are legitimate and legal,* and I defy anyone to prove otherwise.

2. Gaming, or Gambling, is a legitimate business, a big business in the state of Nevada. A legal business.

3. Is there "racket" or Mafia money at work or invested in Nevada? Possibly. I personally don't know

of any which doesn't mean it doesn't exist. It's possible that someone is now running an operation that was built with this kind of money, but we have a Gaming commission in our state that's pretty hard-nosed about such matters, for the very reason you'd expect them to be hard-nosed; they're not a group of stupid men, and they know that the entire world has its eyes on Nevada, just waiting to get in a good, juicy story about rackets and racketeering. I can assure you of this: every effort has been made, is being made and will continue to be made to keep such money out of the state. We don't need it and we don't want it. Naturally, in your mind you'll associate "gambling" with "racketeering," but as I stated, there's little chance for the big-time operators to even come through the *front* door of our casinos, let alone the back door. We even have lists, and admit it, of certain known criminal elements which are not even allowed inside the casinos.

4. If you don't believe me as to how tightly we try to control this sort of thing, just ask Frank Sinatra. He blew his license at Lake Tahoe and the only reason you read so much about it is that it happened to be a big name who was involved. There have been and will continue to be plenty of "busts" for this sort of thing.

5. Another reason you hear so much talk about "gangsterism" and "outside (meaning "racket") influence" is the fact that so many writers will pick Las Vegas as the locale for a crime story involving lots of gang chieftans or "overlords" and staffing the casinos with ex-cons and the like. Well, you can't blame the reader for this. It makes interesting reading and so on, but it *does* give our town a black eye, I'll admit it, and

if they've got to keep on with this sort of writing, why don't you pick on Reno for awhile and give us Las Vegas guys a break? I'll tell you something else. It's better than even money that you've got more gangsters and hoodlum elements in your town than we have in Vegas. We can't afford them, to begin with. In the second place, our casinos are well-policed in addition to our regular city cops. Pull any monkey business here, and away you go, straight to the pokey!

6. This doesn't have a great deal to do directly outside or gangster elements, but remember: we have wives and kids just as you do. We have kindergartens, elementary schools, high schools, churches. We don't want our families and kids subject to the whims or fancies of a bunch of dope-pushers, stick-up artists and degenerates any more than you. We have a simple solution. We don't allow it. We simply don't allow it. Ever hear of a teen-age "rumble" in Las Vegas? You never will. Narcotics is an organized, a highly-organized operation. It couldn't survive in Vegas simply because our town is too well policed. Occasionally, of course, some creep who's "turned on" the junk will hit town, but he doesn't stay long because he can't make a "buy," and has to go elsewhere for his supply.

There's no such thing as organized prostitution in Vegas, and I say this flatly and categorically. I personally know at least two pimps who are doing time for importing girls from Hollywood. We're a broad-minded community, perhaps too much so, but whenever anything smells like "syndicate" or "organization," we root it out fast.

Can you find a girl in Las Vegas? Depends. Depends on can you find a girl anywhere? But if you're thinking of picking up some cute little chorus girl or cocktail waitress, forget it. They mix with their own crowd.

* * *

A FOOL AND HIS MONEY

And you know the rest of *that* old saying. A fool and his money are soon parted. Nowhere in the world is that more true than in the casinos. There's another saying, too: "A little knowledge is a dangerous thing."

Maybe so, but in a casino it's better than no knowledge at all, let me assure you. So read this book carefully. You should get a *little* knowledge from it.

* * *

AN ODD THOUGHT

There's an old saying "White man beat Indian once, shame on White man. White man beat Indian twice, shame on *Indian!*" So if you go into a game without knowledge of the rules and plays you should make, *once,* all right, chalk it up to experience. If you do it a *second* time, then you're a nut!

THE END